THE

DANGEROUS

WIFE

Published in Australia by
Abington Park Media

First published in Australia 2026
Copyright © M.J. Checketts 2026

All rights reserved.

No part of this publication may be reproduced, stored in a retrieval system, or transmitted in any form or by any means, electronic, mechanical, photocopying, recording, or otherwise, without the prior written permission of the publisher, except in the case of brief quotations used in critical articles or reviews.

This is a work of narrative non-fiction. Every effort has been made to ensure the accuracy of historical events, quotations, and sources. All material is based on primary records, legal documents, and contemporaneous press reports.

First published in Australia in 2026 by Abington Park Media

National Library of Australia Cataloguing in Publication entry

 A catalogue record for this book is available from the National Library of Australia

ISBN 978-1-7643582-0-0 (paperback)
ISBN 978-1-7643582-1-7 (hardback)
ISBN 978-1-7643582-2-4 (epub)

Cover design by Aleaca 99 Designs
Book design by Sophie White Design

Printed by Ingram Spark

To receive updates on forthcoming titles, behind-the-scenes research from the legal archives, and early announcements of new releases, email info@mjchecketts.com.

Every reader message is answered personally.

The DANGEROUS Wife

M.J. CHECKETTS

PREFACE

I was close to abandoning the project.

But then the email arrived, and it changed everything.

For months, I'd been researching the trial of Kathleen Fraser, the society wife who shot her husband on a crowded Melbourne street. The century-old case carried every hallmark of a legal thriller—a violent and corrosive marriage, whispers of scandal, and two of Melbourne's fiercest barristers locked in a duel for her life. It raised questions about gender and class that felt startlingly modern. Yet Kathleen Fraser had been completely forgotten. No books, no documentaries, no podcasts.

I wanted desperately to write the book. But there was a problem. I had plenty of secondary material—newspaper articles, dusty law reports, biographies—but no compelling primary source. Without one, I would simply be rearranging the work of others.

Sensing I was at a dead end, my interest cooled. I turned my attention to other things, forgetting I had already ordered digital scans of the Crown Prosecution Brief from the government archives.

When the email finally arrived, I let it sit unopened for a few days. But one idle evening I clicked through to the attachments. Depositions. A witness list. Nothing to set the world alight.

Then I noticed the margins.

Fine pencil strokes ran up the side of each deposition—thin, slanted, perfectly even. They looked like an alien script or a spymaster's code. I recognised them immediately as Pitman shorthand.

I hadn't seen those looping hieroglyphics since my days as a young lawyer in the mid-nineties. Back then I'd watched, agog, as unflappable secretaries took dictation with terrifying speed. Even in those days, the art was dying. Dictaphones had been around for years, but my old-school supervising partner still preferred his secretary to take shorthand. And she was happy to oblige, as it allowed her to refine his meandering monologues right there in real time.

And here it was again, alive in the margins of a Victorian-era prosecution brief. Every deposition was lined with those same delicate strokes. Who had written them? Why? And what did they say?

I sent them for transcription. When they came back a few weeks later, I read the first page and sat bolt upright. This wasn't clerical notation—it was dialogue. The notes captured each witness's cross-examination.

Some exchanges matched the newspapers. Others were new—or disturbingly different. And threaded through the testimony were flashes of what the press had missed or sanitised—the barbed remarks, the pettiness, the small cruelties—details that revealed a marriage far darker than even Melbourne's sensationalist newspapers had dared to describe.

And then it clicked.

Weeks earlier I'd read a stray line in an old newspaper: the Crown Prosecutor, Charles Braine Finlayson, had learned Pitman shorthand to record cross-examinations verbatim in court. I'd smiled at the time. In my day, shorthand was the domain of legal secretaries, not senior counsel. But now I understood. These notes hadn't been written by a clerk.

They were *his*.

In recording the cross-examination of each witness directly onto their respective depositions, Finlayson had ensured that their complete testimony was recorded on the same document. A logical system, characteristic of a meticulous lawyer. What he left behind was a rare thing: a contemporaneous record of a courtroom in full motion. Notes so precise it felt like they were waiting to be found.

His notes changed everything: the evidence, the dynamics, even my sense of who Kathleen Fraser was. The woman who had been reviled, pitied, and admired in equal measure had now stepped out from behind the newsprint.

Pencil marks that had slept for a century had begun to speak again. And what they revealed could no longer remain in the archives.

M.J. Checketts
Melbourne, 2026

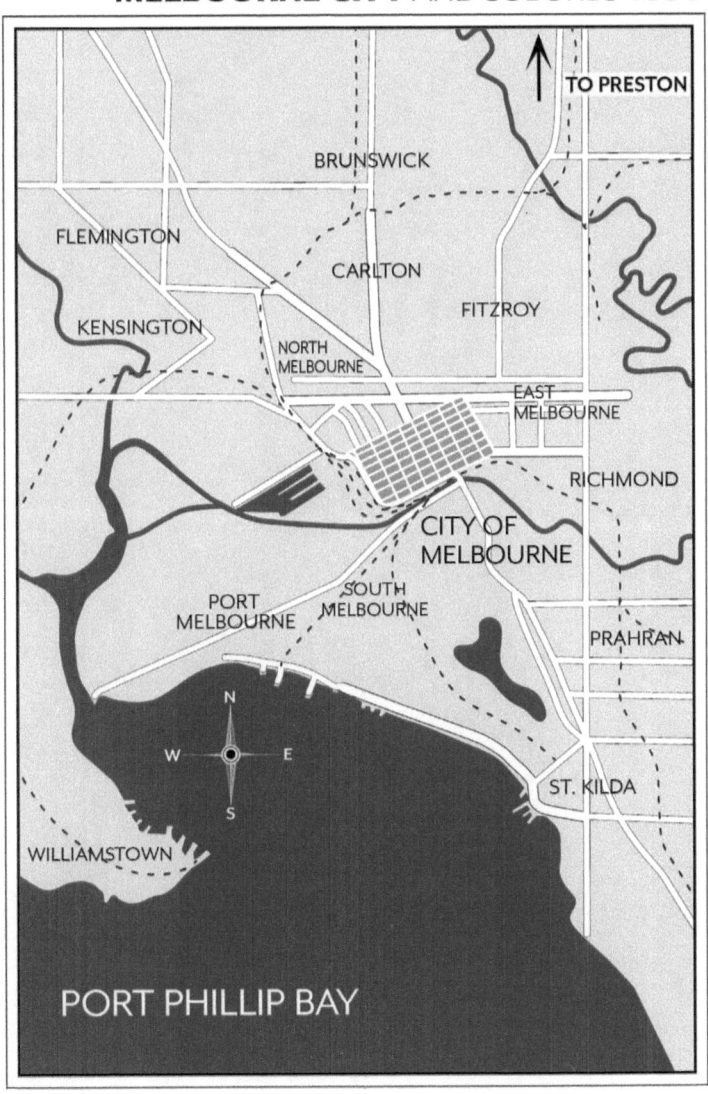

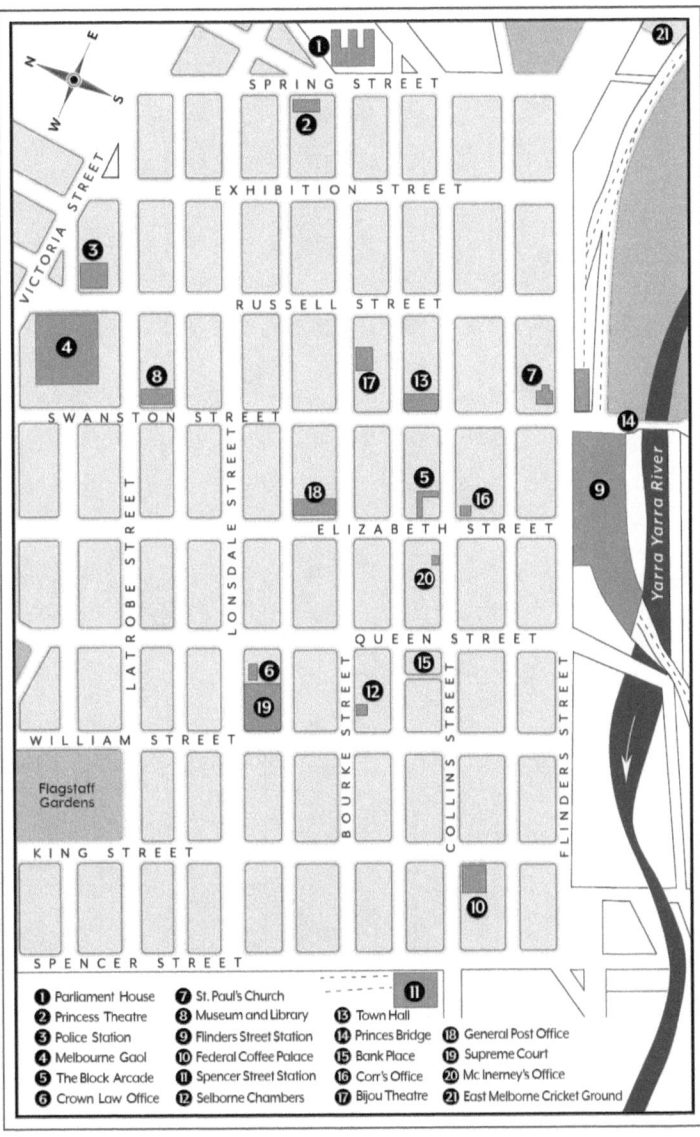

ST.KILDA 1899

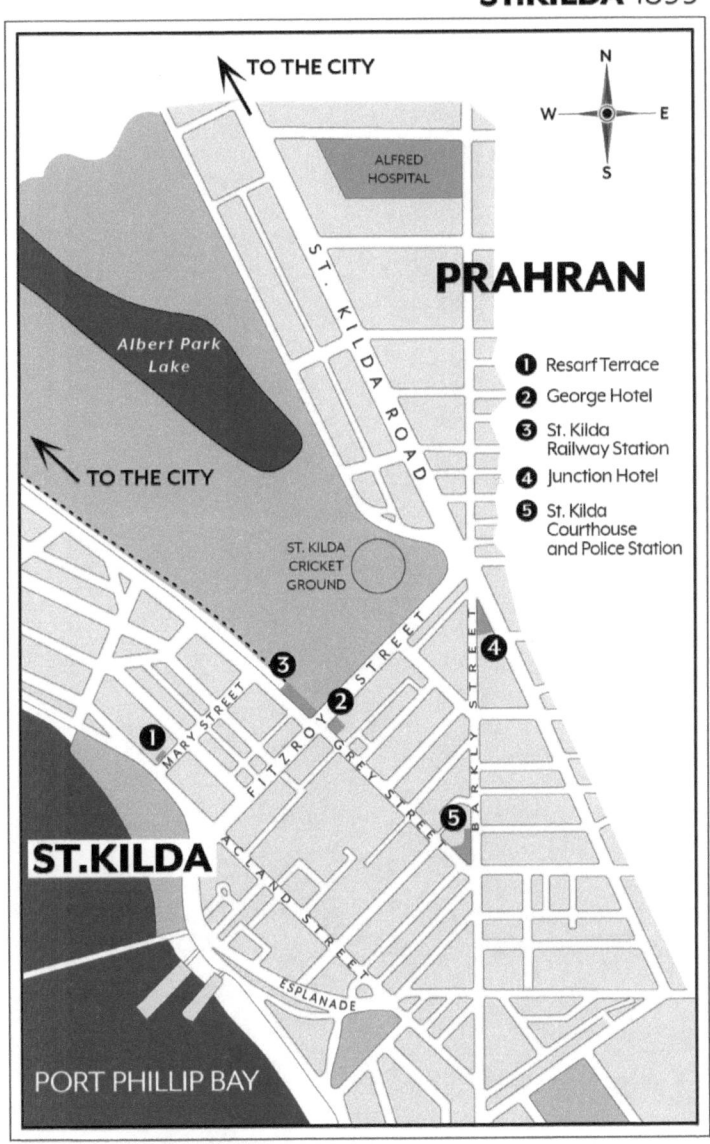

Of all the cases with which I was connected during my long career in the Victorian Police, this, I think, was the most extraordinary.

The complete facts connected with it would assuredly furnish excellent material for a very interesting novel.

Were the circumstances to be related in some place where they could not be verified, many people would probably say they emanated from the fertile imagination of some Baron Munchausen.

A Wife's Dastardly Act: Reminiscences of a Victorian Detective
— DG O'Donnell. *Sunbury News*, 1925

A woman cannot be herself in contemporary society; it is an exclusively male society, with laws drafted by men, and with accusers and judges who judge feminine conduct from a masculine standpoint.

— Henrik Ibsen, *Notes for the Tragedy of Modern Times,* 1878

CHAPTER 1

Wimmera Place, St Kilda, Melbourne – circa 1897

It began, as it so often did, with voices bleeding through brickwork.

Wimmera Place was short and neat, the kind of street where curtains twitched behind cast-iron lacework and respectability hung in the air like scented soap. The smallest sounds carried between the single-fronted terraces: a chair scraping, a kettle filling, a floorboard squeaking.

When Dr and Mrs Fraser rented furnished accommodation there, he with his stiff, proper accent and she with her Devonshire burr, the neighbours soon learned the rhythm of their quarrels. This one was louder than most.

At first, there was only talking. Then shouting. His voice, firm and measured. Hers, high-pitched, persistent. And then a third voice — male, unfamiliar, theatrical. A singing master, someone said later. Teaching Mrs Fraser her scales, or so she claimed.

No one knew what was said, only that it escalated. Furniture scraped, doors slammed. A scuffle. Someone stumbled.

Then the crack. A gunshot, like a riding crop striking leather.

A pause. A breath. The woman screamed. Across the street, an eye glinted through a sliver in the curtain.

By the time a constable arrived the noise had faded, but the questions were only just beginning. Inside the house, no one could, or would, explain what had happened. No injury was reported, although a weapon had clearly been discharged. The other man, the singing master, was gone.

No charges were laid. No statement was taken. The matter was forgotten until two years later, when that same revolver fired again on a crowded St Kilda street.

That time, the bullet didn't miss.

CHAPTER 2

James Liddell Purves QC was Melbourne's best lawyer. Even though he routinely ignored the law.

He mangled precedents, fudged procedures, and treated the rules of evidence like optional extras. Yet time after time, trial after trial, juries followed him like sailors to a siren.

The Press was equally besotted. *The Age*'s coverage of Purves' courtroom theatrics read like a string of love letters. And when he won them the biggest libel trial of the century, their infatuation only deepened.

His critics called him a bluffer. A showboat. A man who played fast and loose with facts and law. But like all charmers, he knew how to close. And he kept on winning.

Resplendent in horsehair wig and silk gown, Purves flicked through his brief, already plotting his first move. His mouth curled at the corners, a perpetual sneer half hidden beneath a thick, well-groomed moustache.

Across the bar table, Crown Prosecutor Charles Braine Finlayson watched him like a playgoer studying a stage illusionist. He knew it was all a trick. But he still couldn't work out what was hidden up the sleeves of Purves' tailored court coat.

Only Queen's Counsel, such as Purves, wore silk gowns. The appointment was known as *taking silk*, a phrase that spoke of prestige, privilege, and power. By contrast, Finlayson—seven years older than Purves—wore a frayed old wool gown, thinning at the seams. It marked him not as a QC, but as a junior barrister. A quiet indignity he bore without complaint as he approached his seventh decade.

As barristers, Purves and Finlayson were opposites. Purves played to the crowd; Finlayson played by the book. Purves was theatrical and intuitive; a courtroom performer, not an academic lawyer. Finlayson, a freemason of the Royal Arch order, was precise and principled. Judges turned to him for guidance on thorny questions of law. His technical mastery would later earn him a seat on the elite taskforce charged with rewriting the Criminal Code.

But in court, Purves beat him. Again, and again.

'Mr Finlayson,' the Court Crier announced. 'You may now open the case for the Crown.'

Finlayson gathered his notes, steadied his hands. This was his moment. He began to rise.

But Purves was already on his feet.

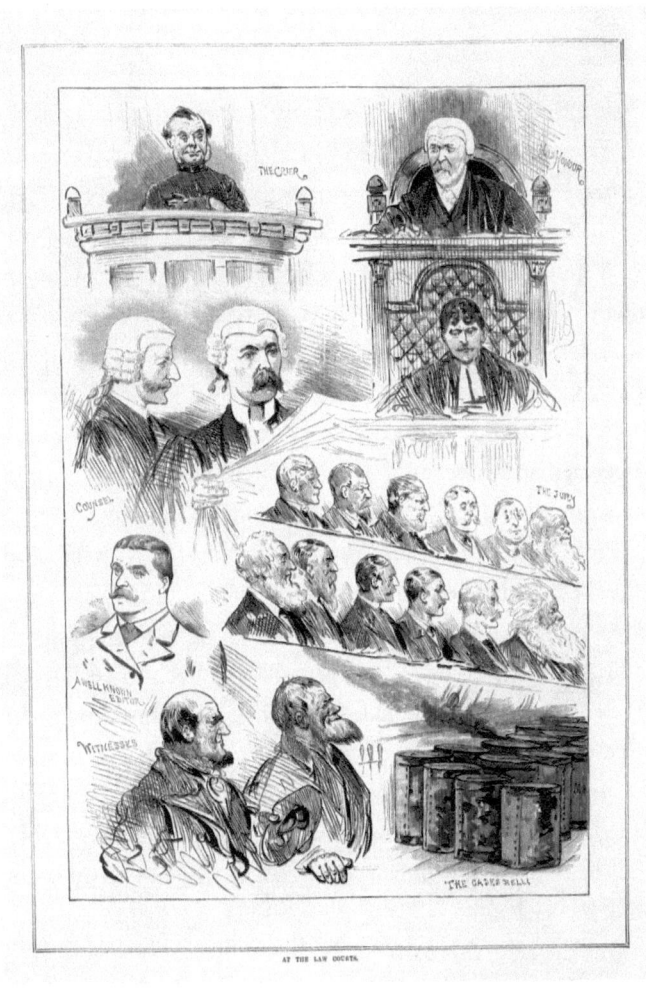

Cartoon: *At the Law Courts* – Alfred Martin Ebsworth, 1887. JL Purves QC featured to the right of the heading 'Counsel'.

CHAPTER 3

He interjected before Finlayson could draw breath.

'Your Honour, might Mrs Sealey and Mrs Fitzjames be permitted to take a seat in the dock?'

Finlayson had seen this trick before.

When defending women, Purves liked to stage an air of fragility. He wanted the jury to see two delicate widows, not two back-street butchers whose bungled surgery had killed a young woman.

Finlayson didn't object. To do so would make him look ungentlemanly in front of the jury. Chairs were brought in and the women sat, heads bowed. Round one to Purves.

Finlayson stood and laid out the facts, bare and unembellished. The courtroom hushed as he told how twenty-three-year-old Alberta Emmeline Jarrett, affectionately known as Miss Bert, had died following an illegal abortion performed by the defendants. Their instruments had been crude, the infection fatal, and three doctors had confirmed it.

On paper, the prosecution should have been straightforward. The law was clear, the evidence unanswerable, and the defence had no witnesses to call. Finlayson laid it out brick by brick.

But then Purves rose.

The leading man had now taken centre stage.

When cross-examining the victim's mother, Purves quickly elicited that she had borne ten children, all of them now dead. Cot death. Tuberculosis. Diphtheria. Measles.

He didn't say it outright, but somehow he conjured the impression that Miss Bert was no more than the last domino in a line destined to fall. That her death said something about the mother herself: her character, her fitness. It made no sense, yet his performance was hypnotic, and logic soon disappeared beneath the shimmer of his mesmeric voice.

Shifting the spotlight to the three eminent physicians who had given expert evidence for the Crown, Purves then suggested that one was a paid zealot who made his living testifying against his peers. It wasn't true, but Finlayson saw a flicker of interest ripple through the jury box. The seed had been planted.

When another doctor's evidence was mentioned—one whose conclusions didn't suit Purves' narrative—he waved it aside. 'I know him,' he said airily. 'I'll go and see him myself.' It was pure theatre, but the jury were now convinced that Purves moved in a world where facts bent to his will, where experts genuflected and changed their testimony at his command.

Purves closed by suggesting that the doctor and a detective had conspired to distort the Crown's evidence. It was pure fantasy, but added one more speck of doubt. By day's end, Finlayson's well-built case lay smeared and skewed by innuendo and half-truths, its once-clear structure now blurred beyond recognition.

The newspapers recorded little of Purves' final speech, only that he claimed the girl had died of a chill. The sort of ailment that might excuse a lady from afternoon tea, not explain the death of a healthy young woman from blood poisoning and pleuro-pneumonia. Yet, from the silver tongue of James Liddell Purves QC, even absurdity acquired the cadence of conviction.

The jury were out for barely an hour.

Not guilty.

Finlayson had prosecuted with reason and restraint, yet once again Purves' performance had eclipsed the facts.

Finlayson had lost the unlosable case.

He stacked his papers in silence.

CHAPTER 4

Thursday 21 September 1899

The chisel came hurtling through the open gate, slicing through the air towards John Grinham's head. He ducked, reflexes taking over. It clattered onto the laneway behind, ringing out against the bluestone.

The other site workers looked on, frozen—tools paused mid-air, eyes wide.

Mrs Kathleen Fraser stood against the jagged outline of a half-built wall, arm still outstretched. Her body shook. Her face twisted with fury.

Just a few feet away, Dr Paul Wilkes Fraser—her husband and the chisel's intended target—lunged at her. He seized her wrists, struggling to pin her down as she writhed and twisted like a trapped animal.

Grinham knew the other workers wouldn't intervene. Especially not the timid William Gordon, who was already edging back, disappearing behind the scaffold.

'Grinham!' both Frasers shouted at once, voices overlapping, raw with urgency.

His stomach knotted. He wasn't a stranger to fights. Back in the bush, he might have leapt in fists first. But here? This was genteel St Kilda. This was different.

He hesitated, gripping the edges of his canvas apron. This was a domestic matter, not his place, not his problem. But Mrs Fraser was flailing, and the doctor's grip was tightening.

Grinham stepped forward. He wedged himself between the raging spouses, pushing hard at the doctor's chest. It took all his strength, but at last he separated them. He stood firm, holding them apart with splayed arms.

Mrs Fraser's chest heaved as she fixed her blazing eyes on her husband. 'You damned cad!' she yelled, voice bouncing off the unfinished walls. 'How dare you follow me!'

She stabbed a trembling finger at him. 'I'll become a public whore if that's what you think I am. Leave immediately! I'll send for a constable!'

'Go ahead,' came the flat reply. He turned and walked away.

Silence followed, thick and unnatural.

She turned to Grinham. Her eyes locked onto his. The rage didn't fade. It shifted, hardened.

'I'll tell you what, Mr Grinham,' she said, voice low and conspiratorial. 'I'll either do for him myself, or find someone who will. I'll do away with him.'

Grinham blinked. Had she just said that?

She took a step forward, blonde ringlets bouncing. 'I've got plenty of money,' she said. 'I can go wherever I please. And, I have the doctor's Will.'

As she leaned in, her voice curled like smoke:

'If he dropped dead at my feet, I wouldn't shed a tear.'

Then came the smile—thin, unholy.

'I'd laugh, and dance on his grave.'

CHAPTER 5

Seconds after making her ominous threats, Mrs Fraser's temperament shifted.

She flipped into a businesslike tone and launched a long monologue about the building project—joinery, mouldings, skirting boards—as though nothing had happened.

Grinham forced himself to nod along.

Resarf Terrace, a five-home development on Mary Street in St Kilda, oozed wealth and status, or at least, it would when completed. Just a stone's throw from St Kilda beach, the playground of Melbourne's elite, the homes would be a world away from Grinham's own modest lodgings in the working-class suburb of West Melbourne.

The Frasers had acquired the vacant land for £2,800, and had already received an offer of £6,000 for the project once completed. Title to the land was in her name, although the couple argued often as to which of them had funded the development costs.

It was rare for a married society lady to oversee a building project, and Mrs Fraser was no mere figurehead. She was the one making decisions, issuing instructions, and handling disputes. In a world where women of her station were expected to preside over tea parties in drawing rooms, her command of bricks, mortar, and payrolls was remarkable.

For Grinham the work was steady, but it came with volatility. The Frasers fought constantly. Only weeks earlier, the site workers had seen her slap her husband with a paintbrush, splattering red paint across his face.

Dr Fraser reappeared at the gate. Grinham tensed.

'What are you doing back here?' Mrs Fraser demanded.

'Nothing in particular,' he replied, his tone nonchalant.

'I suppose you're here to spy on me?'

'No, I'm not. I came back to see Mr Grinham.'

Grinham stiffened.

'What for?' she pressed.

'That's not your business.'

But his wife was undeterred, and her questions came fast and unrelenting. Finally, he faced her with a smug grin and delivered his punchline: 'I'm here to ask Grinham to accompany me into town, to the Federal.'

Grinham gulped. Dr Fraser had just thrown a Molotov cocktail into the bunker.

The Federal Coffee Palace, a grand temperance hotel in the city, was where Mrs Fraser and the couple's young daughter Katie had been living since the Frasers separated some weeks ago. The doctor had become obsessed with the place, convinced his wife was entertaining other men there, although he had no proof. At least, not until recently. Grinham and the others had witnessed it. Mid-argument, she'd turned to her husband and snapped, loud enough for every worker on site to hear: 'If you come to the Federal any night, you'll see someone lying in my bed where you should be.'

A confession? A taunt? Grinham couldn't tell. Either way, Dr Fraser had lurked around the Federal Coffee Palace ever since, badgering staff with his endless questions. And now he was dragging Grinham into it.

Grinham knew this was a chess move. And he was the pawn.

Mrs Fraser's expression darkened. She turned to Grinham,

her eyes narrowing. But when she finally spoke, the explosion never came. 'If you would like to go,' she said, flipping her golden curls with theatrical disdain, 'you can do so on your own responsibility.'

Tradesmen like Grinham weren't used to defying men like Dr Fraser. Convention demanded a lowered gaze and quiet obedience. Whatever sympathy he might have felt for Mrs Fraser, the social order left little doubt about where the authority lay. A wife, no matter how spirited, was expected to yield. A tradesman, doubly so. To cross a man of standing was risky. But to side with his wife against him was to upend the natural order of things.

Grinham didn't meet her eye. With a reluctant shrug, he agreed to accompany her husband to the Federal.

CHAPTER 6

9.55 am, Saturday 23 September 1899

Edwin James Corr stifled a yawn as his elegant mahogany chair seemed to swallow him whole.

He'd already been navigating a labyrinth of legalese for two tedious hours, and the clock had yet to strike ten.

Still, there was pride in it. Pride in the brass plate on the door. Pride in the crisp printed letterhead. Corr's father, a grocer, had scrimped and saved to send him to Melbourne's prestigious Scotch College. Corr had repaid him by graduating dux of the school and elbowing his way into the ranks of the city's elite.

Aged just thirty-three and a bachelor, Corr was a young law firm partner, although his prematurely balding scalp lent him a gravitas beyond his years. Messrs. Corr and Rylah handled deeds and documents, wills and estates, real estate transactions, bankruptcies, criminal cases, and, of course, lawsuits. Their offices at 285 Collins Street, between Elizabeth and Swanston in the heart of Melbourne's bustling commercial district, placed them right in the thick of things.

Just sixty years earlier, this grand thoroughfare of gothic revival banks and neoclassical offices had been virgin bushland, alive only with the tread of Wurundjeri hunters and the thump of kangaroos. But now, on the cusp of the twentieth century, Collins Street danced to the relentless rhythm of commerce.

Corr and his business partner Walter Rylah practised law as *Amalgams*. In other words, they practised as both barristers and solicitors.

Edwin James Corr c.1904

Traditionally, following the English model, the legal profession was divided into two distinct branches. Barristers, the upper branch of the profession, were specialist advocates who appeared in the higher courts garbed in wigs and gowns. Senior barristers were handed the key to the corridors of power when appointed Queen's Counsel or QC. Prestigious, clubbable, and small in number, the Melbourne bar was populated by upper class gentlemen with big brains and bigger egos. Many of them, like Finlayson and Purves, had trained in London at one of the medieval Inns of Court.

Solicitors formed the lower branch of the profession. They were office men, briefing the barristers and undertaking non-court work such as conveyancing, establishing companies, and drafting wills. Unlike barristers, solicitors were allowed to work together in partnerships, known as law firms. When all was said and done, the hierarchy was clear: barristers strutted around like kings, and solicitors scurried along behind them.

Amalgamation was a recent colonial innovation, designed to create efficiencies and reduce legal costs. Or at least, that was the theory. In practice, little changed because the old order fought back. Barristers closed ranks. They mocked, blocked and blackballed any Amalgam who had the temerity to stray onto their patch. Wolves, after all, don't campaign for stronger fences.

No one howled louder against amalgamation than James Liddell Purves QC. He famously scoffed that amalgamation would 'enable a man who has failed in one profession to fail in another also. If he has mistaken his profession as a barrister, he will be afforded the opportunity to mistake it again by becoming a solicitor.'

And so, despite the best intentions of the legislature, the status quo endured. The top barristers still took their pick of the lucrative briefs in the Supreme Court, and the top law firms secured access to their talent by confining their practice to a traditional solicitor's role. The Amalgams, mainly small law firms and country practitioners, operated outside this cosy club, with decidedly mixed results.

Incidentally, Purves' reference to 'a man' in his celebrated speech was no mere generality. There were no women in the ranks of either branch of the legal profession.

A clerk poked his head around the heavy oak door.

'Dr Fraser is here to see you.'

Collins Street, 1890s

CHAPTER 7

Two days earlier, Dr Fraser had contacted Corr's office to rewrite his Will. A clerk took down the basics and scheduled an appointment.

At precisely ten o'clock, Fraser returned.

Corr studied him with a practised eye. The man's collar was soiled, his hair uncombed. His overall appearance was … unsettled. For a moment, Corr wondered if he'd been drinking. But no—this wasn't alcohol. It looked more like neglect. Fraser had the air of a man who'd stopped taking care of himself.

Fraser introduced himself with clipped British tones, intimating they had met before. For a moment, Corr couldn't quite place him. Then he remembered.

'The Junction Hotel, last Queen's Birthday,' Corr said, quick as a flash. 'After the bicycle races at St Kilda Cricket Ground.'

Fraser had looked different that day, sharper, cleaner, more in command. He'd been there with his wife, Kathleen, who had peppered Corr with endless questions about the races. Corr would later describe her as 'garrulous.' Fraser, taciturn and irritated, had tolerated her chatter with clenched civility.

Junction Hotel St Kilda c.1900

Professionally, that day had been a win for Corr. Not only had he met Dr Fraser, but he'd also picked up a tidy little personal injury case for William Martin, thrown off his bicycle by arch-rival Laurence Corbett. Melbourne's great sporting events were fertile hunting grounds for the legal profession, full of well-heeled clients and prospects. Collins Street lawyers hovered like crows over a sheep station, and that day Corr had been one of many in the circling flock.

Fraser didn't linger on pleasantries, telling Corr he had

a lunchtime appointment in St Kilda. So Corr got straight down to business, leading his new client through the usual questions about his assets, liabilities, funeral plans, executor, and the like. Fraser threw out his answers rapid-fire, seemingly without much thought. But when Corr asked him about his beneficiaries, the mood shifted.

Fraser's eyes fixed on the lawyer without blinking. In a deliberate voice, Fraser made himself clear: upon his death, every possession, every asset, and every scrap of value he owned was to go directly to his father in Wolverhampton, England. And if his father predeceased him, it was all to pass to his three sisters back in England. No exceptions.

A cold shiver crept up Corr's spine. 'What about Mrs Fraser?' he asked, keeping his tone neutral.

Fraser looked away.

CHAPTER 8

The question hung in the air a moment too long.

Fraser sighed, rubbing a hand over his face. 'We haven't been getting along these last three years.'

Corr nodded, his pencil scratching across the page in a slow, unbroken rhythm. He asked no questions and offered no opinion. But Dr Fraser's decision to disinherit his wife was the kind of instruction that tended to attract questions. Sometimes even lawsuits.

Mrs Fraser, as Corr had observed at the races that day, didn't seem like a woman easily cowed. She had the bearing, confidence, and vocal stamina of a *New Woman*. One of those bloomer-clad radicals who took to litigation like a suffragist to a soapbox. If disinherited, she might sue. Technically speaking, the law was still on Dr Fraser's side, but the winds of change were blowing hard.

Under the *Married Women's Property Act* of 1884, wives now had the right to hold property in their own names. Women in New Zealand had been granted the vote six years ago, and here in Victoria they were campaigning for the same rights. And in South Australia, the progressive Parliamentarian King O'Malley had recently proposed a new law to force men to leave part of their estate to their widows.

Corr could see that Fraser wasn't in the mood for a lecture about estate risk, so he kept things efficient. He asked a few more questions, made a detailed file note, and moved on. There would be an opportunity to re-write the Will in a year or two, if the law continued to shift. Legislative change was good for business, and it was a beautiful thing when a client's legal interests aligned so squarely with his lawyer's commercial ones.

Fraser mentioned a letter from his wife's lawyer, demanding the payment of money from some mining shares that had been sold. The money had been paid to him instead of her, and she wasn't happy about it.

'She never had any money other than what I gave her,' Fraser scoffed. 'I'll just ignore the letter.'

'I'd advise against that,' Corr replied. 'Ignoring it could lead to complications down the road.' What those complications might have been, Corr didn't specify. But that wasn't the point. What *was* important, was that he had bought himself some more backside insurance.

Corr finished taking Fraser's instructions and got to work preparing the Will. Meanwhile, Fraser paced the waiting room like a man spring-loaded, checking his watch every few minutes.

Corr drafted the Will longhand on a sheet of vellum, and handed it to his clerk to type up on the Remington. The Remington Standard typewriter was now clawing its way into every law office on Collins Street. It wasn't just a machine; it was a revolution in black metal and brass. Where clerks once toiled with pen and blotter, the Remington delivered clean, crisp prose in minutes.

The clerk attacked the Remington with practiced precision, the machine responding like an obedient metal workhorse. Within minutes, the document was created. Fraser hovered restlessly as Corr checked it line by line. By noon, he handed Fraser the finished product. Fraser signed without hesitation. Corr then filed it in his fireproof cabinet, and gave Fraser a certified copy. Corr presented his invoice, and Fraser wrote out a cheque on the spot.

Corr had worked fast and billed faster. And if things turned ugly later, his backside was bulletproof, thanks to those copious file notes.

CHAPTER 9

12.20 pm, Saturday 23 September 1899

John Grinham walked up to the site office at Resarf Terrace. The name, Fraser in reverse, had once seemed charming. Now it seemed like a bad joke about their backwards marriage.

He'd been summoned by Mrs Fraser. Likely, he thought, to clear the air. His recent visit to the Federal Coffee Palace with her husband had been awkward and, as it turned out, entirely unnecessary.

Mr Smith, the manager, had greeted them with professional neutrality. No, he said, his staff had observed no impropriety, no unfamiliar men, no after-hours visitors. Nothing had changed, Smith confirmed, since the last time Dr Fraser visited. Or the time before that. If anything, Smith added with a wry grin, Mrs Fraser was the perfect guest, quiet, self-contained, always polite.

When Grinham entered the cramped office, Mrs Fraser was already waiting. He offered a diplomatic smile, just the right blend of professionalism and deference. Surely they could put this behind them and move on?

Her expression stopped him cold.

No greeting. No preamble. The words came out like spit:

'Well, now you have deserted me and gone on the doctor's side.'

Grinham opened his mouth to explain, to apologise, to say anything. But her hand was already up. What he'd done had cut deeper than betrayal. It had reinforced a system built to silence her.

'You are a pair of damned cads!' she snapped. 'You can go! You've done yourself out of work through going in with the doctor.'

He tried again to speak, but the words caught in his throat.

She was already moving. Her full skirts swept the dusty floor as she turned, disappearing through the doorway without another glance.

She hadn't paid him. She hadn't even paused. It was over.

Five minutes later, Mrs Fraser was marching off to Grey Street to meet her husband.

There was dirty business afoot.

CHAPTER 10

1.00 pm, Saturday 23 September 1899

The periodicity of their reproductive life, with its accompanying physiological crises, renders women more liable to mental derangement.

— H. Maudsley, *Sex in Mind and in Education*, 1874.

Just over an hour after Dr Fraser left the city offices of Corr and Rylah, the ink barely dry on his new Will, Senior Constable Antony Joseph Trainor was patrolling his beat in St Kilda.

Melbourne's famed seaside suburb combined residential elegance with bustling leisure. Once a tranquil rural settlement, the arrival of the railway in 1857 had transformed it into a prestigious locale, with grand mansions lining Fitzroy Street, Grey Street, and Acland Street. When the first edition of *Bourke's Colonial Gentry* was published in 1891, ten out of just seventy Australian families authorised to use heraldic crests lived in St Kilda.

In the twilight of his forties, Trainor was a twenty-four-year veteran of the Victoria Police who would be promoted to Sergeant within weeks. He cut an impressive figure with his full flowing beard and dark blue uniform buttoned to the neck. His domed helmet, black and unyielding, crowned a figure that brooked no nonsense.

Crossing Fitzroy Street from the train station, Trainor moved through a shifting tide of well-dressed men and women, all drifting between grand hotels, terraced mansions, and high-end boutiques. The air was a pungent mix of horse manure, swirling grit, and sea salt from the bay. Shop windows gleamed with silks, French millinery, and Swiss timepieces.

A gust of wind rolled up the dusty thoroughfare from the beach, flinging grit into his eyes. Trainor lifted a gloved hand to shield his face. With its dry heat, unpaved roads, and sea breezes, dust storms were a common occurrence in St Kilda.

At the corner of Grey Street, the George Hotel loomed up out of the haze like a dream in plaster and glass. Its whitewashed walls gleamed in the sun, its parapets and bay windows almost too delicate for the harsh Antipodean light. With a bit of imagination, and the dust cloud around it, one could fancy it the colonial approximation of a fairytale palace rising out of the morning mist, its whimsical dome as opulent as any that might be seen in the finest cities of Europe.

The George Hotel St Kilda c.1900

Embedded in the hotel's ground floor along the Grey Street frontage sat a row of refined shops. Their stone façades and tall windows whispered wealth.

Trainor's eyes fell on a man and a woman, huddled together in the doorway of one of those shops. The sign above the door read *AH Fishley – Jeweller*. The man's collar was wrinkled and stained, and his hair unkempt. The woman, in contrast, was prim and polished, her curly blonde hair perfectly coiffed under an expensive hat. Trainor didn't recognise either of them. He wondered why they were standing next to a closed door, but then he realised that the doorway offered a degree of shelter from the scudding dust cloud.

Trainor marched past the pair, noticing that they were engaged in an earnest, but not heated, discussion. He put his head down and continued his patrol up Grey Street.

Barely a heartbeat passed before Trainor heard a loud and unmistakable sound behind him…the ringing retort of a handgun.

CHAPTER 11

Trainor's body reacted before his mind had time to catch up. He spun on his heel, instinct taking hold. The gunshot echoed down the street. Screams rang out. People scattered. He sprinted back toward the George.

Trainor's eyes were fixed on the man who had been standing in the doorway. Now he was on the ground, holding his temple and groaning in pain. A stream of blood flowed from the fallen man's head, already staining the doorstep a deep crimson. Nearby, his freshly filled tobacco pipe lay untouched on the ground.

And then Trainor saw it.

A pocket revolver lay glinting in the sunlight on the dusty road. A thin trail of smoke slithered upwards, merging with the swirling red dust as if the earth itself had exhaled. Sulphurous gunpowder filled Trainor's nostrils, mixing with the dry heat of the dust. The woman stood over her fallen companion, speechless and unmoving. Her face was frozen, her complexion now as white as the rendered walls of the George.

A boy from the crowd stepped forward, picked up the revolver, and handed it to the policeman with a swagger. Trainor held the still-warm weapon in one hand, whilst guiding the woman through the now-open shop door.

'Who fired the shot?' Trainor demanded.

'I did it, I did it!' the woman gasped, the gentle lilt of her Devonshire accent strangely at odds with the panic in her voice.

'Who is this man?' Trainor pressed.

'My husband.' she replied.

'Who is your husband?'

'Doctor Fraser is his name,' she whispered, 'and I am Mrs Fraser.'

Trainor looked back and forth between the shaken woman and the injured man.

'I'll have to arrest you.' he said, taking her by the arm.

'Don't hold me, I won't run away.'

Could he trust her? Respectable women didn't shoot their husbands in broad daylight unless they'd already gone past the edge. For all he knew, there was another gun, or maybe a blade, hidden in the folds of her dress. If she turned violent again, he might not have time to react, and if she bolted, he might lose her. But the man, her husband, was bleeding out on the doorstep, his frock coat darkening with each pulse.

Trainor knew what a crowd like this could become. Memories of an unruly mob in Ballarat years before were seared on his mind—the man leaping out of the crowd, and the cold bite of steel as the knife split his scalp. *'Go for the Bobby!'* they'd screamed. Trainor still bore the scar. He scanned the street, then the shop. Faces everywhere, but no help. Just gawking, screeching, like a flock of startled galahs.

The victim needed pressure on his wound, and fast. Trainor levelled the woman with a firm gaze. 'Sit down and don't move,' he commanded. She obeyed.

He rushed to the injured man. Taking a handkerchief from Fraser's own pocket, Trainor fashioned it at lightning speed into a makeshift bandage, and pressed it hard against the wound. Fraser groaned, barely conscious. Trainor cursed. He needed to move fast.

Meanwhile, Mrs Fraser had found her voice. She kept

repeating, 'I did it!' at high decibels to anyone who would listen, her voice then raising to a yell, 'I'll get hung for it. My God! My God! He maddened me to it! I wish to God that I were dead!'

Trainor's eyes scanned the street for help. He shouted for someone to flag down a hansom cab, and within minutes one arrived, rattling to a stop in a cloud of dust.

True to her word, Mrs Fraser hadn't moved an inch. She now knelt next to her husband, wailing, 'forgive me for shooting you.'

Trainor hoisted the injured man to his feet and walked him to the cab, each step heavy and awkward, but he succeeded in lifting the man inside. Mrs Fraser hovered nearby. 'You too,' he ordered. She climbed in beside her husband. 'To the St Kilda lockup,' Trainor shouted to the cabman. With a clatter of hooves, they were off along Grey Street.

Inside, Mrs Fraser turned to him. 'Do you believe in fate?' she asked, her eyes fixed on his with unsettling intensity. Before he could respond, she spoke again with the mystical cadence of a fortune-teller. 'I believe in it. There's always something urging me on to do things that I cannot resist.'

Trainor looked away. He had no reply.

They arrived at the St Kilda Police Station, on the corner of Grey and Barkly Streets, within minutes. Trainor escorted the woman from cab to building. He handed her over to the watchhouse keeper, Senior Constable George Doran Williams, and instructed the Station Clerk to summon Detective O'Donnell. He then ran back outside to the cab.

He opened the carriage door, and recoiled.

CHAPTER 12

The darkest deeds are done in the light of day, beneath the cover of propriety.

— Fergus W. Hume, *The Mystery of a Hansom Cab*, 1886

The arrival of a prone man in a hansom cab at the St Kilda Police Station was a bizarre echo of the most celebrated fictional crime of Melbourne's short history.

The Mystery of a Hansom Cab by barrister Fergus W. Hume was published in 1886. Set in Melbourne in the mid-1880s, it was one of the world's first detective novels. The book sold a massive 100,000 copies in its first two Australian print runs, and went on to become a runaway success in both Britain and America. It even outsold Arthur Conan Doyle's first Sherlock Holmes novel, *A Study in Scarlet*.

The opening hook of the novel, with which most Melburnians were familiar, involved a hansom cab driving up Grey Street and arriving at St Kilda Police Station, with a murdered man on board. From that intriguing beginning, the novel peeled back the veneer of propriety upheld by Melbourne's upper classes. Many of the wealthy characters were found to be hiding secrets that could ruin their reputations. In contrast, Hume's hansom cab driver and other working-class characters provided a dramatic foil to the opulent lives of the rich. *The Mystery of a Hansom Cab* ended with justice being served, but not before the moral decay and hypocrisy of Melbourne's ruling elite had been exposed.

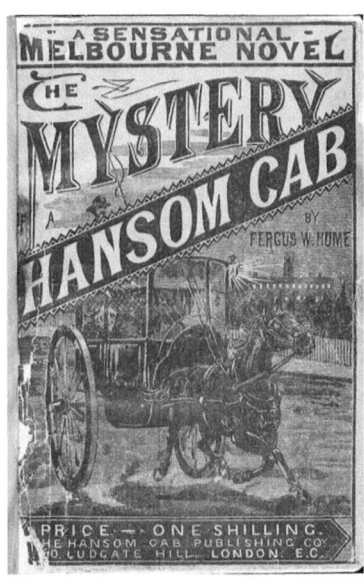

But on that Saturday afternoon in St Kilda, Senior Constable Williams wasn't thinking about literary parallels. This wasn't fiction. There would be no final scene where all is revealed. Just a man bleeding out in the back of a cab, and a city that preferred its scandals swept beneath the rug.

When Kathleen Fraser stepped through the station doors, something in Williams' gut clenched. He had never met her before, but he knew things about her. Things that now crowded the front of his mind and refused to budge.

He sat Mrs Fraser down in the interview room. Even as his pulse hammered in his throat, his training took over. 'I'm sorry to hear what's happened,' he said.

'Yes, it is a bad job, but I did it,' she replied. 'I shot him in the temple.' She started to cry, her sobs shallow at first, then ragged and convulsive. She looked up at Williams with red, puffy eyes. 'I don't mind what they do to me, but for the sake of my child, I do pray he will get better. Do you think I shall be hanged?'

Williams knew the answer. The law was clear: the death sentence was mandatory for the crime of murder. If her husband died, she would swing for it. And even if he survived, the charge would likely be attempted murder. The penalty was the same. But he couldn't tell her that. Not yet. Not now. Instead, he offered something soft-edged and useless. 'Hope for the best,' he muttered.

She nodded, clasping her hands together as if in prayer.

Sweat prickled under the stiff blue collar of Williams' tunic as he leaned back and cleared his throat. 'With luck, his injury won't be serious,' he ventured.

She clutched at the words like a drowning woman.

'So, Mrs Fraser,' he continued, forcing his voice into something resembling casual detachment, 'is there a particular reason for all this trouble?'

Her words came out in a rush. 'It was a letter... from a woman... back in England.' She paused, her eyes darting to the floor, then back to him. 'It was addressed to my husband.'

Williams leaned forward, focusing. This wasn't the response he had expected. 'And what did the letter say?'

Her lips tightened and she wrung her hands together, the tension radiating off her. 'The letter insinuated that they had a child together. An illegitimate child.'

Williams fought hard to keep his expression neutral. 'How long ago did you find out about this?'

Her voice was low now, almost trembling. 'It was some months ago. I didn't want to believe it at first, but after I saw that letter...' Her gaze darkened, the fire returning, '... everything changed.'

Williams inclined his head, eyes steady. 'And that's when the trouble between you started?'

She nodded.

He watched her for a moment, letting her words sink in. There were always two sides to every story. But the question hung there, heavy and unresolved: *What was he supposed to do with the side he already knew?*

St Kilda Courthouse (left hand side / centre) and Police Station (far right hand side)

CHAPTER 13

Trainor's breath caught in his throat as Dr. Fraser sank lower into the seat of the hansom cab.

Fraser's face was now ashen and twisted. A violent spasm shook him, then he stopped moving altogether.

Trainor barked at the cabman, insisting on top speed to the Alfred Hospital. The man cracked the reins, snapping the horse into motion.

It was a short ride. When the cab pulled up, Trainor leapt down and helped Fraser to alight. To his relief, Fraser's colour had returned and his voice steadied.

As Trainor helped Fraser through the main portico, the hush hit like a wall. The air was cool, still, and faintly antiseptic—a world away from the heat, wind and dust of Grey Street.

Alfred Hospital, Melbourne, Victoria in 1881. State Library of Victoria

Fraser appeared stable as he walked toward the reception desk, drawing no more attention than any other ambulant patient. Trainor allowed himself a glimmer of optimism. Maybe this wasn't as dire as he'd feared.

A moment later, his hope dissolved into crimson and bile as Fraser's body stiffened. His face went white. Then, with a sickening wet gurgle, he started to wretch and puke. As the greenish vomit bounced off the floor and sprayed up the pristine white walls, the stench that followed was rank and sour.

'Help him!' Trainor shouted, lunging forward to catch Fraser before he collapsed.

A matron strode over, her features carved in permanent disapproval beneath an elaborate white cap. 'Dr Hearne, quickly!' she called.

Fraser swayed, clutching his head. Blood began to stream down the side of his temple, catching the light as it dripped onto the floor.

Dr William Weston Hearne arrived within seconds. Aged just twenty-eight and with a thin frame, striking moustache, and shadowed eyes, he carried a quiet intensity that belied his inexperience. Gunshot wounds were rare at the Alfred, although treating them was an expertise that Hearne would develop later in other theatres. Eyes wide and uncertain, Hearne crouched beside Fraser and examined him.

William Weston Hearne (middle, left)
with Alfred Hospital nurses 1903

Trainor gave a short, urgent explanation. The young doctor nodded, trying to make sense of a situation he knew was above his pay grade. 'Please could you call Doctor O'Hara?' he asked the matron, with the air of a green subaltern trying to give orders to a battle-hardened sergeant-major. But her sturdy black shoes were one step ahead of him. She was already marching off to find a real doctor.

Trainor stood helpless as Hearne fumbled to stabilise the patient. Things were going downhill fast.

The heavy doors at the far end of the room burst open, and a towering figure strode in. At over six feet tall and with broad shoulders, Dr Henry Michael O'Hara was one of the colony's finest surgeons. A trained opera singer and former heavyweight boxing champion of Trinity College Dublin, he was as famous for his baritone and his right hook as he was for his surgical brilliance. Hearne shrank back to make space.

O'Hara's instructions came rapid fire, spurring the nurses into action. Moments later, an orderly appeared with a wheeled stretcher rattling at speed. With practised authority, O'Hara directed the transfer to the operating theatre.

With Fraser in capable hands, Trainor didn't wait. He burst back through the hospital doors, the heat and glare of Commercial Road hitting him like a slap.

A cab clattered past. He lunged into the road, waving it down with both arms.

There was work to do—and not a moment to lose.

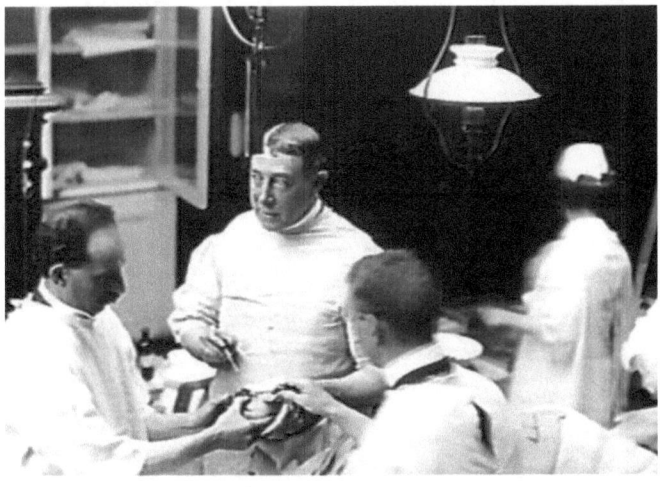

Dr Henry O'Hara at the operating table – Museums Victoria

CHAPTER 14

With the letter from England off her chest, Mrs Fraser's breathing steadied and the colour returned to her cheeks.

Seizing the moment, Williams asked if he might take her statement. She nodded. He dipped his pen in the inkwell and began to write, taking it down word for word:

You must know that we have been living apart for some weeks.

After our separation, I and my little girl, who is eight years of age, went to reside at the Federal Coffee Palace, and my husband remained at the boarding house in St Kilda. I was anxious about my little girl and resolved to put her in the Kew convent. That resolve I carried out a few days ago, and then I wrote to my husband requesting that he should make some provision for her maintenance and education. As the result of that letter, we met by appointment in Grey Street.

We had no sooner met than we began to quarrel. He accused me of being a whore, and followed up that statement by asserting that even then I was cohabiting with another man. That made me very angry, and I indignantly repelled his charge. He only smiled, and then we had a dispute about the child, which increased my anger, and I said, 'If you say I am a whore and that our child is not your child, I will prove myself so from this time forth.' 'You can do your best,' said he, and as he spoke, he put his pipe in his mouth and got ready to light it.

Then I put my hand in my pocket, pulled out a revolver which I had carried for years, and shot him through the temple.

Williams paused, lifting his pen. If the court accepted Mrs Fraser's version of events, she might yet inspire sympathy. Women faced severe social stigma for perceived promiscuity, and men faced similar consequences for falsely accusing them. The word *whore* was not to be bandied around lightly.

When the newspapers reported Mrs Fraser's statement the following week, they substituted the euphemism: *lewd woman*. Even in print, the original word was too potent to repeat.

Illegitimacy also carried a profound social stigma, particularly amongst the upper classes. In *The Mystery of a Hansom Cab*, villain Oliver Whyte discovered that young society lady Madge Frettlby was illegitimate. Her father, a powerful businessman, had gone to great lengths to conceal the truth and protect her social standing. Whyte's blackmail, the enormous sum of £3,000, reflected just how ruinous Madge's exposure was perceived to be.

Mrs Fraser signed her statement, then sank back into her chair. She had given Williams a full account. Or so he believed.

Later, when the courtroom was packed and all of Melbourne was watching, she would tell her story again. But for her second performance, she would rewrite the script.

CHAPTER 15

Get your facts first, then you can distort them as you please.

— Mark Twain, 1889

Detective David George O'Donnell strode past the matron and flung open the door to the operating theatre.

Behind him came the procession of Detective Bannon, Senior Constable Trainor, Mrs Fraser, and one of the local magistrates, Justice Moore.

The room, now full to bursting, remained a flurry of activity. Nurses checked gleaming instruments. The X-ray technician prepared his machine, a shiny, brass-limbed contraption that O'Hara treated as reverently as a priest handling the chalice. O'Hara was Melbourne's loudest evangelist for the new technology, having lobbied hard for the Alfred to purchase the machine the previous year.

O'Donnell announced himself in a mongrel Irish brogue. He explained that they were there to take what was known as a Dying Man's Deposition from Dr Fraser.

O'Donnell was hard to miss. Standing tall at six foot two, he weighed a massive twenty stone. With his strong track record, steely ethics, and a heart as big as his fists, he was the closest thing Victoria Police had to a celebrity detective. As a young copper, he'd been hand-picked for the elite team that hunted down notorious bushranger Ned Kelly. He'd also received an award for bravery. When dressed in full uniform, helmet and handcuffs, he'd once dived off a pier into the raging sea to save a drowning woman and her child.

With a few words, O'Donnell persuaded O'Hara to allow the deposition. The doctor, a seasoned expert medical witness, understood the necessity, even if he would have preferred to get straight to surgery. And in any event, Fraser was now refusing to succumb to the X-Ray machine. Perhaps a brief distraction wouldn't hurt.

Under section 193 of the Justices Act 1890, a Dying Man's Deposition could be taken when a witness was unlikely to survive until the committal hearing. The same procedure had been used to obtain the evidence of Miss Bert Jarrett in the abortion murder trial of Seeley and Fitzjames. It required several formalities: a magistrate present; a medical opinion that death was likely; and, crucially, the accused must be allowed to question the witness. Because if the witness were to die before the hearing, there would be no further opportunity for cross-examination.

O'Donnell knew that this Dying Man's Deposition had to be handled just right. Legally, it had to be airtight. His oversized boots squeaked on the tiled floor as he walked over to the wounded man, filling the space with quiet authority.

Mrs Fraser broke down once more at the sight of her wounded husband. Her cries echoed off the bare walls, as if the room itself might shatter. O'Donnell tried his best to ignore her as she clutched her skirts and wailed. He knew she had to be there. If she were excluded, the deposition would be defective and not admissible in evidence.

O'Donnell positioned himself near Fraser's bed, his heavy presence looming. He beckoned the magistrate over, along with Hearne and O'Hara. Mrs Fraser's voice cut through the air once more, the repetitive 'Oh my God!' jarring like nails on a chalkboard.

It was O'Hara who finally snapped. 'Any outbreak of excitement on your part may mean the death of your husband,' he said, voice low but firm. *And in turn, make you a murderer*, was his clear but unspoken message.

'I will be quiet, yes, I will be quiet,' Mrs Fraser replied. O'Donnell would later write 'notwithstanding her promise, she did not control herself.'

Detective Bannon ushered Dr Hearne towards the magistrate. Following Bannon's prompts under O'Donnell's watchful eye, the young Registrar stated under oath that Dr Fraser was dangerously ill and unlikely to recover. They all then gathered around the wounded man. O'Donnell asked the questions, and wrote down every word:

My name is Paul Wilkes Fraser. I am a surgeon and physician, living in Grey Street, St Kilda.

Kathleen Fraser, now present, is my wife. She lives apart from me. She has lived apart from me for about a month. She lives at the Federal Coffee Palace. We mutually agreed to part on account of disagreements. I have seen her about half a dozen times during the past month, generally at the corner of Mary and Park Streets, St Kilda.

I saw her some time about 12 or 1 o'clock today near Hampton House. We had some arguments concerning private affairs. There was an explosion or report, and the next thing I remember I was sitting on the pavement. There was no one with me. A constable came along, put me into a cab and brought me to the Alfred Hospital. I cannot say what became of my wife after the explosion. I was too stunned to remember anything. There was blood on my face, pouring down, when the constable came. The constable bandaged my forehead. I remember my wife being driven with me in the cab to the St Kilda lock-up. She didn't come with me to the hospital in the cab.

I did not see a revolver with my wife today. I did not know she had one. I never had a revolver at any time.

She was in an excited mood today when she met me. She was in my company about 10 minutes. She did not threaten me in any way. I did not say anything to provoke her. I can give no reason why she should fire at me or injure me. I gave her no provocation.

We have been married about nine years. We were married in England, in Plymouth. We have been in this colony about four years, and were in Tasmania and New South Wales previously. We have quarrelled on previous occasions.

There is nothing further I would like to add.

There was then one final step to complete. With deliberate and practised formality, O'Donnell asked Mrs Fraser if she had any questions for her husband, or matters of clarification.

Mrs Fraser stalled for what seemed like an eternity. At last she said, 'My husband does not want to say anything more, so I think I had better not.' And then she crumbled.

Collapsing into a heap of tears, her voice cracked with desperation. 'Please, Paul, don't die... for our child's sake.' she pleaded, her words ricocheting off the sterile walls like the report of her handgun just hours before.

'I want to live for my own sake,' her husband muttered.

Fraser swore the oath before Justice Moore, who countersigned, recording the date, place, and names of each attendee.

The policemen took Mrs Fraser, still teary-eyed and unsteady, back to the St Kilda Police Station. Before Mr Moore, they charged her with the attempted murder of Dr Paul Wilkes Fraser. A cab was summoned to take her to the remand wing of Melbourne Gaol.

On the steps of the Police Station, she turned to Trainor. Her hands trembled as she dug into her bag and pulled out a set of keys. 'To my room,' she murmured, 'at the Federal Coffee Palace.' She had pre-empted his request.

Detective David George O'Donnell

CHAPTER 16

*The worst crime is the one which
comes dressed in respectability.*

— Fergus W. Hume, *The Mystery of a Hansom Cab*, 1886

O'Donnell and Trainor made their way to the Federal Coffee Palace at 555 Collins Street, a few blocks down from the law offices of Corr and Rylah.

A cornerstone of Melbourne's temperance movement, the Federal was a dry hotel. Coffee Palaces had sprung up all over the city in recent years, offering respectable alternatives to the booze-soaked pubs that dotted every block.

The Federal Coffee Palace

But the Federal was no ordinary Coffee Palace — it was one of the most opulent hotels in the world. Built in 1888 with no less than five million bricks, it had 560 rooms and a façade so ornate it nearly buckled under its own ambition.

As they drew near O'Donnell and Trainor might have gawked at the stern stone griffins guarding the edifice, but it was the statue of Venus in her chariot, drawn by four rearing seahorses, that crowned the spectacle. The Federal wasn't just a hotel; it was a cathedral to capitalism.

When the Federal was built, confidence in Melbourne's future seemed without limit. That decade of wealth and prosperity would be remembered as the *Marvellous Melbourne* period. O'Donnell and Trainor had seen the boom at its height: new railway lines snaking across the city, theatres glittering with electric light, office blocks with hydraulic lifts climbing skyward on Collins Street, and grotesque suburban mansions stuffed with gaudy furniture.

And then they had seen it all come crashing down. In 1892 the land companies collapsed, the banks slammed their doors, and men who had staked a lifetime's savings on Melbourne real estate were left to wander the streets as beggars. No building captured the extremes of that period more completely than the Federal.

Walking through the grand front doors, the policemen entered a soaring four-storey atrium where light filtered down through the glass roof in watery shafts. As their boots clicked on the marble floor, a faint whiff of roasted coffee beans drifted down from the mezzanine. They presented their credentials. Mr Smith, the manager, led them upstairs to Mrs Fraser's room.

Grand Lobby, Federal Coffee Palace

When Smith unlocked the door, the heavy latch gave a long creak that echoed down the corridor. Stepping inside, the room exuded opulence—velvet rugs, upholstered chairs, and a heavy wardrobe overflowing with fine garments.

Smith explained that Mrs Fraser's young daughter had lived with her here until Wednesday last week, when she had placed her in a convent in Kew. That timing gave cause to pause. It seemed too recent, too convenient. Was it evidence of premeditation?

Then came the incongruous detail: a tandem bicycle leaning at an odd angle in the corner.

'She and the doctor used to ride it together,' Smith explained, 'Since the separation, they've been fighting over it. He came to collect it last week—I turned him away. He said, "It's mine, and I can prove it," and stormed off.'

The officers began their search. No cartridges were found to match the revolver, but they did uncover several items of interest.

Fine jewellery was stashed at the back of the wardrobe. More was held in a tin box in the hotel's safe. There were various photographs of Mrs Fraser, and another of a gentleman whom Smith said had also recently stayed at the Federal Coffee Palace. If there had been an affair, it left no trace beyond that single image.

Then they found the tin trunk.

It was heavy. Black. Inside were papers, folders, blueprints, certificates, syndicate agreements, leases, and prospectuses for speculative Tasmanian mining ventures. The names of fledgling companies danced before their eyes. Many of them had Mrs Fraser's signature at the foot of the page.

Trainor let out a low whistle. This woman wasn't some passive investor. She was running operations, raising capital, structuring deals. And she was visiting the mines herself— doing the due diligence, staking claims, putting her balance sheet to work.

Looking at the cache of mining documents, O'Donnell and Trainor may have recalled myriad newspaper articles that exalted Mrs Fraser's bold forays into mining speculation over the last few years. One particularly saccharine puff piece from the *Zeehan and Dundas Herald*, headlined *A Lady Speculator*, had praised her ability not only to navigate the difficult terrain of Mount Read, Ringville, and Rosebery, but also to entertain the miners with singing concerts when she got there. She so captivated one miner at Colebrook that he wrote an epic poem in her honour. Another once offered her the last of his food, telling her, 'I could live for a day on your smiles.'

As they put the mining papers back in the tin trunk, Mr Smith lingered at the threshold. 'There's something else,' he said. 'The doctor's been here often. Twice he stayed overnight but in a separate room. He'd come in asking questions. Prying.'

O'Donnell scratched a line into his notebook and shut it with a snap.

The pieces were shifting, slowly but surely, into place.

CHAPTER 17

On Monday 25 September 1899, the front pages of *The Age* contained the usual densely-packed adverts for steamship fares, ladies' apparel, situations vacant, items for sale, and bicycle repairs. Next came dispatches from the motherland. Page three confirmed what Melbourne had been expecting for some time: the British were shipping fifty thousand men to the Transvaal. War against the Boers now seemed inevitable.

Then, there it was. The headline on page five screamed in large font:

TRAGEDY AT ST KILDA. A DOCTOR SHOT BY HIS WIFE. BULLET IN THE HEAD. HIS CONDITION SERIOUS. AN EXTRAORDINARY STORY. FINANCIAL DISPUTES AND JEALOUSY.

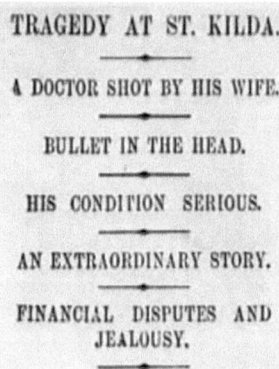

The article told of a volatile marriage between a 'passionate, impetuous woman' and an 'unyielding, obstinate man.' They had fought for years, and had separated a few weeks before the shooting incident.

Readers were stunned to learn that on the very day of the shooting, Dr Fraser had signed a new Will, cutting his wife out completely.

It wasn't the first time shots had been fired. Two years ago, there had been another incident between the couple. A Singing Master had been visiting Mrs Fraser at their home, supposedly for music lessons. The doctor had been suspicious. He had thrown the man out and then, according to an alarmed neighbour, a gunshot was heard. The Constable sent to investigate got no straight answers from the couple, confessing that he never got to the bottom of the matter.

One fellow lodger at Hampton House, the genteel boarding house where the couple had been staying, described Mrs Fraser as *bright*, *vivacious*, and *very hysterical*. Her husband was described as *brooding*. The couple fought loudly and often. One night, Mrs Fraser had screamed for help. Fellow lodgers rushed to find her standing in the hall, terrified.

'He'll kill me.' she said.

One of them ran inside. Fraser sat, pipe in hand, unmoved by the commotion.

'What's the matter?'

'Oh, nothing,' the doctor had replied, 'My wife threw a lamp at me and screamed. You'll find the pieces in the corner.'

On another occasion, suspecting his wife of infidelity, Fraser had trailed her to the Bijou Theatre on Bourke Street. He bought himself a ticket in the dress circle, and spied on his wife and her companion in the stalls below. She spotted him immediately. Turning the tables, she introduced her husband to the other man during the interval. By the end of the night, the two men were seen drinking together.

Bijou Theatre, Bourke Street

Senior Constable George Doran Williams also disclosed what had been on his mind that afternoon when Mrs Fraser was brought into the St Kilda Police Station. He told *The Age* that, just days before the shooting, Dr Fraser had come to him seeking advice. The two men were friends. Fraser confided that he and his wife 'led a wretched married life' and had recently separated. He said Kathleen was now living at the Federal Coffee Palace, and that she had 'resolved to warrant his suspicions' of infidelity.

Williams told him the police wouldn't intervene in private matters between husband and wife. He recommended hiring a private investigator. When Fraser dismissed that idea, Williams suggested he also rent a room at the Coffee Palace, to keep an eye on her comings and goings.

Anonymous sources had plenty to say. Dr Fraser, they claimed, was due to inherit a fortune from family in England. Mrs Fraser, for her part, was a mining speculator, and unusually successful at it. Some said she had helped her husband make thousands from shares in Mount Lyell, the largest and most lucrative copper mine in Tasmania. The couple were said to be so involved in the mining industry they had built an assaying laboratory in St Kilda, complete with imported English machinery. Fraser apparently locked it up like a fortress day and night, paranoid about theft.

But money hadn't brought happiness. 'I've heard her complain of mistreatment' said one unnamed source. 'He said she was delusional' claimed another. 'He treated her himself, and was certain of it.'

And yet, even this revelation ended on a note of tenderness. 'After one particularly nasty row,' the anonymous man continued, 'I asked the doctor why they stayed together. "Ah," he told me, "we could never separate for good. I can't live without her, and I'm fully convinced she can't live without me".'

Melbourne *Punch* – 28 September 1899

Mrs. Fraser, of the St. Kilda Shooting Case.

Australian Town and Country Journal – Sydney NSW,
Saturday 14 October 1899

CHAPTER 18

When James Liddell Purves QC read the newspaper reports about the Fraser shooting, it must have felt like déjà vu.

A spurned woman.

A loaded pistol.

A man accused of betrayal.

And a jury, waiting to be swayed.

He had seen it all before.

Nearly twenty-five years earlier, aged just thirty-one, Purves had stood in a rural courthouse defending another woman charged with a crime of passion. Her name was Phoebe Post. Her alleged victim: a man who had seduced her, abandoned her, and left her with child. When he began openly courting another woman, Miss Post snapped. She confronted him with a pistol. Her shot missed, but not by much. And for that, she faced the gallows for attempted murder.

It would be the case that launched his career.

A young barrister with a lion's mane of dark hair, he had little experience but no shortage of confidence.

The courtroom was packed. The crowd was tense. And Purves ignited the room like kerosene on kindling.

In a move that would become his signature, he asked the judge to allow Miss Post to sit in the dock. A touch of gallantry, a touch of theatre.

Purves called no witnesses. Instead, he dismantled the seducer, Edward Donnelly, piece by piece. At the end of his lengthy cross-examination the man practically crawled out of the witness box on his hands and knees.

Then, with the crowd hushed, Purves rose for his closing.

The speech he gave was legally shaky, but rhetorically sublime. The press gushed from every corner of the colony. Overnight, James Liddell Purves became the barrister of choice for wealthy defendants who needed to dazzle a jury.

Purves had studied the Greco-Roman rhetorical masters with a passion he had never shown for legislation or caselaw. He revered Demosthenes, the greatest orator of ancient Athens, who had argued that persuasive speech must blend logos (logic), ethos (credibility), and pathos (emotion). Demosthenes was known for his pace, his precision, and the rhythm of his prose. Purves absorbed these concepts and made them his own. He didn't argue a case—he performed it. And here was his chance to shine.

In his impassioned speech on behalf of Phoebe Post, Purves leaned into every classical rhetorical technique available. His attack on Edward Donnelly—'this licentious, lecherous, crawling creature'—employed *assonance* and *alliteration* to create a lyrical rhythm that was simultaneously poetic and savage.

He continued in a similar vein: 'I will tell you the real story, for my client's lips are closed. They were sealed by that nuggetty-framed and lecherous creature; that bush Hercules, all body and no mind.' Here, Purves combined *ethos* and *pathos* to devastating effect. His client's silence became a moral virtue, her ruined reputation the real victim.

Using the rhetorical technique of *epimone*, he deliberately hammered out the name 'Edward Donnelly' time and time again. Each repetition was a metronomic blow, until the mantra became a cudgel, and the cudgel crushed its target.

Like Plato's charioteer, Purves didn't just engage the white horse of the jury's reason. He also yanked hard on the reins of the black horse of emotion. He made them feel, and not just see, his client's desperation. When Purves finally sat down, the entire courtroom erupted in spontaneous cheering. The applause was cut short by attending policemen.

Taking his courtroom chivalry one step further, Purves then persuaded the judge to let his client wait comfortably in an adjoining room while the jury deliberated.

The verdict? Not guilty.

From that day, Purves was not just another toffee-nosed Melbourne barrister. He was the demi-god who had talked a jury into forgiving a woman who pulled the trigger.

Had Finlayson been in court that day, he wouldn't have risen with outrage, nor sought to match Purves flourish for flourish. But he might have stood, calm and composed, to remind the jury that behind the polished rhetoric, Purves had misrepresented both the law and the facts.

Phoebe Post hadn't been silenced by Edward Donnelly. She had, on Purves' own advice, exercised a defendant's right to silence. A tactical decision, nothing more.

Finlayson might also have pointed out that Purves casually invented facts that were never raised in evidence. He claimed in his closing speech that Miss Post was defending herself from a sexual assault by Donnelly. Or, that she'd succumbed to temporary insanity. It didn't much matter which. There was no evidence of either, but that didn't stop him from pleading both, straight-faced, as if he were reciting from the court record. Nobody ever called him out for it. James Liddell Purves was now invincible.

A quarter of a century later, reading about the shooting in

St Kilda, Purves would have recognised the terrain. Domestic turmoil. A passionate woman. And just enough ambiguity to work his magic.

Purves wasn't allowed to advertise his services. That was forbidden by the Victorian Bar. Tout for business, and you'd soon find yourself the subject of a professional complaint.

But Purves didn't need to tout.

The Fraser brief would come to him.

Just as they always did.

James Liddell Purves QC

CHAPTER 19

St Kilda prided itself on a certain gleam of gentility.

Its mansions, hotels and boarding houses spoke of money. Sometimes old, sometimes new, but always anxious to be displayed.

Its gardens and shaded promenades were a living theatre of the better classes. On bright afternoons, ladies floated along the Esplanade under billowing parasols, their skirts stirring in the sea breeze. Some wore gowns dyed in the vivid new hues of the age: peacock blue, garnet red, or plum bloom. Fashionable hats were tilted at careful angles, pinned with ostrich feathers or a spray of artificial violets.

St Kilda Baths, early 1900s

When the Frasers first arrived there around 1896 they rented furnished accommodation in Wimmera Place, later the scene of the shooting incident with the mysterious Singing Master. Then they moved into a boarding house — the preferred accommodation for wealthy widows, retired officers, and those who wanted flexibility without the burden of running a grand home.

On the surface, the Frasers' life in St Kilda followed the expected forms. They attended concerts on the pier, walked the Esplanade on golden afternoons, and took tea in drawing-rooms where the conversation was as artfully balanced as the bouquets on the side tables.

But difference soon told. When out and about in St Kilda, Mrs Fraser was noticed not just for riding a bicycle, but for having the audacity to do so wearing bloomers. To some, it was a mark of spirited independence; to others, a challenge.

Cycling aligned Mrs Fraser with a broader social current: the rise of the *New Woman*. The term referred to educated, independent, and socially progressive women who were breaking free from Victorian constraints. The New Woman cycled. She travelled. She wore bloomers. She smoked cigarettes in public. The New Woman refused to accept her place as solely ornamental or subordinate. She was admired, resented, and feared—fascinating to the men who watched her, yet threatening to the world they controlled. 'She actively seeks new experience,' one commentator warned, 'and intends to have some impact on the world around her.' That description fitted Mrs Fraser to the inch.

But behind the parasols and polite smiles, the fractures

were already appearing. For a woman like Mrs Fraser—clever, restless, ambitious—St. Kilda's rigid social codes and her husband's curmudgeonly ways wove together like a noose tightening inexorably around her throat.

The manager of Hampton House, the boarding house where they lived immediately before their separation, confirmed that things hadn't ended quietly. He told the press that Mrs Fraser had 'a loud voice' whereas her husband 'seldom spoke more than six words to anyone.' Usually, when tempers frayed, the Frasers had the good sense to take their arguments out onto the street, beyond the damask walls and listening ears. But that final time, they argued indoors. The manager asked only Mrs Fraser to leave. Not the man who simmered in silence, but the woman who dared to be audible.

The next day, she moved to the Federal Coffee Palace.

CHAPTER 20

Tuesday 26 September 1899

At that point, the case was McInerney's. No whispers. No rivals. No interference from bigger names with silk gowns. As far as Dr Thomas Patrick McInerney knew, no other lawyers were circling. Not yet.

He'd handled the Frasers' legal affairs for the last eighteen months. When Kathleen Fraser was arrested, she wrote to him at once from Melbourne Gaol. And now, with the gallows looming and money no object, she was about to become client royalty.

In terms of pure brainpower, McInerney was a cut above the average Melbourne lawyer. His natural intelligence, combined with a voracious appetite for academic study, made him a formidable opponent in court and at the negotiating table.

Born in 1854, amid the feverish chaos of the Bendigo goldfields, McInerney's childhood was a blur of tent towns and shifting fortunes as he followed his father from one gold rush to the next. But even in those rough-and-tumble days, the boy stood out. As soon as he could, he left the diggings behind for the polished halls of Melbourne University. There, he excelled. Later, he founded his own law firm with his younger brother, Tim. The McInerney brothers soon discovered that real wealth wasn't buried in the ground, it was invoiced in retainers and brief fees.

A barrister and solicitor, not a medical man, McInerney had earned his Doctor of Laws through extended postgraduate study. He wore his Doctor prefix like a shiny badge of honour. His higher degree set him apart from the pack, and signalled his ongoing ties to academia. Alongside his bustling Collins Street practice, McInerney occupied the lofty office of Warden of the Senate at his alma mater. It was a prestigious role, with the collateral benefit of unfettered access to Melbourne's ruling classes.

When they met at Melbourne Gaol on the Tuesday following the shooting, McInerney was shocked by Mrs Fraser's appearance. A pale shell of the vibrant woman he knew, her face was drawn, her eyes puffy. She took one look at him and burst into tears.

'Tell me he won't die,' she wailed. 'Give me some hope that he will live, and that my child will not be fatherless.'

After more sobbing, and perhaps raising a dainty hand across her furrowed brow, she moved into a mindset of complete denial. 'Shoot him? God, no!' she insisted. 'I would much rather have shot myself!'

Those who knew McInerney often joked about his inability to suppress a laugh, especially during tedious University Senate meetings. His face would redden, lips tightening, shoulders twitching with the strain of suppressed mirth. Whether the urge struck him in that moment of high melodrama in a prison cell, with a woman's life on the line, is a matter for conjecture.

The Fraser case would do wonders for his profile. She was already the talk of Melbourne. But McInerney knew this wouldn't be an easy defence. Whatever extenuating circumstances he might argue, the facts were unrelenting. His client had been found standing over a smoking gun and a prone body, shouting, 'I did it!' A workman had heard her threaten to kill her husband just two days earlier. And, if that weren't enough, she'd told a constable that she believed in fate, which sometimes led her to irresistible urges beyond her control.

Commercially speaking, it was a dream brief. But legally? A nightmare.

McInerney rubbed his forehead, already turning over the possibilities, weighing the angles, anticipating the arguments he would need to dismantle.

It was time to put his top-notch brain to work.

CHAPTER 21

The one charm of marriage is that it makes a life of deception absolutely necessary for both parties.

Oscar Wilde, *The Picture of Dorian Gray*, 1891

On the same day McInerney visited Mrs Fraser, *The Age* published new details that deepened Melbourne's growing fascination with her case. A series of letters, traced back to London, suggested that Dr Fraser's life was rather more complicated than it appeared.

The tip-off had come from Mrs Fraser herself. On the day of the shooting, she told Senior Constable Williams that her husband had been receiving letters from England. Letters that had troubled her. Reporters followed the lead. Their reward was a cache of correspondence addressed to Dr Fraser from two senders. Louie, a mysterious woman, and Dorothy, a young girl attending Ellerker College in Richmond Hill. Adverts in the *London Standard* described it as a '*high-class school for girls,*' complete with refined touches like riding and swimming lessons.

The first letter was crammed onto a single sheet of notepaper and written in a spidery hand. It started: *Dear Peter*, being Dr Fraser's nickname. The letter read as follows:

Nov 4th 1898

Dear Peter,

I have been asked by my little pet to send this letter on to you which I trust will reach you safely & find you well &

having plenty of good luck and happiness. I was awfully pleased to get your letter from the ship. I would have liked to have answered it but as you required me not to write before hearing from you of course I didn't.

Do and I are most anxious to get a few lines from you, haven't much news for you so I will wait. Mother, Mr A, sisters, join me in sending this love & good wishes for the coming Xmas, Breezie is wonderfully well + getting on splendidly at that school.

Believe me to remain your true friend,

Louie

The second letter was written in the neat handwriting of a child, widely spaced and in straight, deliberate lines. It spanned two pages, as follows:

Ellerker College
Richmond Hill
October 20th 1898

Dear Doctor Fraser

I hope you are quite well and happy. I expect you will think me very unkind not to have written before but I have had such a lot of people to write to. I like this school very much the girls and Governesses are very kind to me. Mother sent me a lovely birthday cake and I enjoyed it very much. They let me have a little party in the evening last Tuesday, and last Monday we all had a little festivity, and two more little girls sang and I did too. I shall be very pleased to see you.

Now I must say goodbye. I am very sorry I cannot say any more so I must end my little letter because I have got to do all my lessons now because this evening we are going to have dancing. I must say good-bye once more.

With heaps of love and thousands of kisses
From your loving Dorothy

Under the child's handwriting were a couple of more lines in Louie's distinctive scrawl, as follows:

What do you think of this? It has been entirely written on her own, no coaching.

Mrs Fraser, increasingly uneasy about the secretive tone of these letters, confronted her husband. Louie was just a friend, he claimed. But if he thought she'd swallow that, he didn't know her at all.

On 11 June 1899, she placed the following advertisement in the London publication *Lloyd's Weekly Newspaper*:

The letter sent from London to Dr Paul Wilkes Fraser, Melbourne, Australia, by person signing herself Louie, and girl signing herself Dorothy, at Ellerker College, Richmond Hill, Richmond, near London; the wife of Dr Paul Wilkes Fraser has said letter. If said person will communicate with Mrs Fraser, it will be greatly to her advantage.—G.P.O., Melbourne, Australia.

It was a strategic move, not voicing her suspicions outright, but baiting Louie with the promise of 'great advantage.' She didn't go through her lawyer. She didn't ask permission. She just made it happen.

Neither Louie nor Dorothy replied.

CHAPTER 22

The power of the lawyer is in the uncertainty of the law.

— Jeremy Bentham

As he mulled over Mrs Fraser's case, McInerney knew that the so-called Dying Man's Deposition sworn by Doctor Fraser was problematic for his client.

Dr Fraser's deposition had given little indication of his wife's state of mind when she shot him. And nothing of provocation. Without such evidence, what conclusion could the jury reach other than that she made a premeditated attempt to murder?

The deposition had to be attacked. Discredited. Or at least…clarified. But how?

McInerney's first thought had been to take a procedural approach. Yes, O'Donnell had given Mrs Fraser the opportunity to ask questions of her husband for the deposition. However, scared and intimidated, and wanting to show due deference to Dr Fraser, she had declined. Had a lawyer been there to protect her interests, he could have asked the right questions. Should her husband die now, his client might lose that opportunity forever. He had already made this point when he wrote to the Crown Solicitor seeking a copy of the deposition, but it was a weak argument, and he knew it. O'Donnell had covered his bases well.

Then, as he mapped the angles in his mind, a bold plan started to form. An approach so creative that it had never been tried before in the Colony of Victoria. An approach that edged close to the line, but stopped just short of crossing it. The kind of genius that makes an expensive lawyer worth every penny of his outrageous fee.

McInerney grabbed his well-worn copy of the Justices Act 1890 from the bookshelf, thumbed through to section 193, and smiled.

CHAPTER 23

McInerney's plan was brilliant in its simplicity. He would secure a *second* Dying Man's Deposition, one that would be more useful to his client's defence.

All he needed was to convince a magistrate to officiate, and a doctor to say that Fraser was still at risk of dying. That claim, however, was becoming harder to sustain. The newspapers were now reporting signs of improvement, even though O'Hara had failed to remove the bullet from Fraser's skull.

There was also the concern about witness tampering. He wouldn't put his professional standing at risk for this plan, however brilliant it was. But then an exquisite thought struck him. Dr Fraser had yet to be subpoenaed by the Crown so, technically speaking, he wasn't currently their witness. He was fair game for anyone.

McInerney wasted no time in manoeuvring magistrate Thomas R. Andrews into officiating. Why Andrews? No one knew for certain. Maybe it was their shared ties to Melbourne University, or maybe it was the deference that Andrews, a school headmaster, might show to a lawyer with McInerney's high academic credentials. Or maybe Andrews just saw the favour for what it was: a loaded chip in the unspoken poker game of professional quid pro quo.

Whatever the connection, Andrews got right on board, professing that the process was sufficiently bulletproof to stop a Gatling gun. 'All the requirements of the law were scrupulously fulfilled.' he later assured the press. He brushed aside Mrs Fraser's absence at the deposition, claiming that McInerney had 'carefully guarded her interests.' Whether

Andrews had cared to ask who was safeguarding the Crown's interests was left unasked, and unanswered.

Dr Fraser had been in better health the last few days. Perhaps for this reason, McInerney stacked the deck further by asking young Dr Hearne, not the more experienced O'Hara, to sign off that he was dangerously ill and unlikely to recover. Whether McInerney knew it or not, Hearne's mind was also now on other things. He had volunteered for South Africa as a military surgeon, and the following week would be granted six months' leave of absence from the Alfred Hospital.

At Fraser's bedside, McInerney went to work. Before the formal questioning even began, Fraser freely volunteered that he had every confidence in his wife's fidelity. He also admitted to having called his wife names when he was angry. In a surprising twist which seemed to ignore his recent history of surveillance, Fraser then claimed that it was in fact his wife, not himself, who was the jealous one in the marriage.

The Argus reported that Fraser 'stood the ordeal of examination splendidly, and all his replies were tinged with sarcastic humour that is rare in a witness in perfect health.' Andrews concurred that, 'it was hard to separate the evidence from the comment, for his fund of sarcasm seemed inexhaustible.'

To McInerney's delight, Fraser opened with a golden nugget: 'I remember last Saturday, 23rd September. I want to make a statement that in my opinion my wife was not in the full possession of her senses that day nor had she been for some days previously.' It was dynamite, blowing a gaping hole in the Prosecution's case.

But he didn't stop there. McInerney pressed Fraser further,

nudging him toward contradictions in his earlier testimony. Where Fraser had once insisted he'd never owned a firearm, he now casually admitted the opposite. 'I did own a revolver,' he told McInerney. 'A small pocket one. She took it. I've no doubt about that. She's a funny kind of woman; as soon as I get a thing, she wants it.'

The revelations were now coming thick and fast. Fraser, resolute in his first deposition that he'd said nothing to provoke his wife, now hedged. He admitted telling her that he saw no point in living with her, and that he was planning to sell up and disappear. He conceded that he *might* have said, 'You can damn well do what you like,' but on reflection, he thought it was unlikely. He also *might* have called her 'a damn liar.' The word *damn*, of course, being blasphemous and a slap in the face of propriety. And, he *might* have also called her a whore ... but he didn't recollect.

By now, McInerney could surely taste victory. The deposition was a masterpiece, chock full of concessions that would turn the case on its head. He'd charmed the witness, lined up the magistrate, and leveraged the young doctor into rubber-stamping the questionable prognosis of imminent death. The prosecution's case might even collapse before trial. Visions of academic law journal plaudits may already have been forming. *The McInerney Deposition,* they'd call it.

But then Fraser ruined everything.

CHAPTER 24

Fraser looked up from the bed, his sharp sarcasm giving way to something else; pain, regret, perhaps even desperation. His bloodshot eyes fixed on McInerney, Hearne, and Andrews as they gathered close. 'I want the three of you to do the best you can between you for her,' he said, his voice soft but steady. McInerney nodded, offering his best empathetic smile, while calculating how to steer the deposition back on course. But Fraser kept talking, and the room turned to ice.

'If you give me the tip to alter my evidence, I will,' he said, each word measured. 'It's no relief to me to give her six months. I'd sooner see her with none at all.'

The weight of it landed like a thunderclap. McInerney froze, jaw clenched. Andrews' pen stopped mid-stroke. The young Dr Hearne looked as if the floor might give way beneath him.

In one sentence, Fraser had smashed his credibility beyond repair. He'd admitted, under oath and in the presence of a lawyer, a doctor, and a magistrate, that his testimony was negotiable.

And there was nothing McInerney could do about it.

CHAPTER 25

In the remand wing of Melbourne Gaol, Mrs Fraser's voice was as relentless as the sun pounding the outside of its grim bluestone walls.

'What will happen to my little girl?' she asked the warders more than twenty times a day. Her desperation, cloaked in the incessant chatter of a voice the press described as 'very loud,' struck a chord even with the toughest of gaol warders. As the *Geelong Advertiser* put it, 'The condition of the woman is altogether pitiable.'

Unlike convicted prisoners, Mrs Fraser enjoyed certain privileges. She wore her own clothes, she was spared from prison labour, she exercised alone and was kept from the general population. Solitude did little to tame her loquacity. She often pressed for news of her husband, and spoke endlessly about her daughter's future.

At first, Mrs Fraser refused to see visitors, including her sister Mrs Howard, who had travelled from Sydney. She told the warders, and later even close friends, the same thing: 'I prefer to be left alone. I want to see no one.'

Within her self-imposed isolation, her voice found a new ritual. A broken incantation, like a dark parody of Aladdin's lamp: 'In my present troubles, there are only three things I want,' she chanted, her West Country cadence turning the phrase into a half-prayer, half-performative lament. 'To be assured that my husband does not think I contemplated his murder, to know that he does not believe me unfaithful, and to be certain that our child will be well looked after should the worst happen.'

As the long prison days wore on, Mrs Fraser's health deteriorated. She ate little, and the hard prison bed left her sleepless. Her cries for her husband and child echoed down the corridors at night. By Thursday, her sixth day of incarceration, the gaol physician moved her to the hospital wing, diagnosing her with 'nervous prostration.' A label often applied to women deemed too fragile to cope.

The timing was convenient. That same day, McInerney announced that Mrs Fraser would plead insanity. At first, he had suggested to the press that Dr Fraser, if he recovered, might take the blame on his own shoulders for having provoked her. But now his position was evolving.

'Evidence will be forthcoming,' reported the *Geelong Advertiser*, 'to show that as far back as two years ago, her sanity was seriously questioned by those who knew her intimately.' McInerney claimed to have well-authenticated statements of 'extraordinary doings on her part' such as pelting a workman at Resarf Terrace with bricks, and hurling broken wood onto the head of another.

Insanity defences weren't unusual for women. The same cultural instincts that labelled them irrational or hysterical could sometimes be turned to their legal advantage. But an insanity acquittal came with its own sentence; indefinite confinement in a lunatic asylum.

By Friday, Mrs Fraser's condition had improved, and she began to receive visitors. When Mrs McCormick, a visiting friend from St Kilda, reassured Mrs Fraser that her husband's condition was improving, she exclaimed 'Thank God!'

Her relief gave way at once to a flood of words. During the entire visit Mrs Fraser spoke only of her husband, her voice rising and falling with emotion. 'If they would let me go to his bedside only for a few minutes, I know we would be all to one another again,' she said.

By contrast, the newspapers deadpanned that Dr Fraser made no enquiry whatsoever for his wife or their child.

When McInerney visited again, he could scarcely sit down before the questions began: 'How is he? Is he better? Does he forgive me? Does he withdraw the horrible charges against me? Will he live to look after our child?'

The *Herald* was merciless: 'Like a woman she ran on,' they reported, 'asking questions, but never waiting for an answer.'

Outside the gaol, Mrs Fraser's mental state soon became fodder for public discourse. Dr O'Hara, apparently unconcerned with patient confidentiality, told the press that he had once treated Mrs Fraser and found her 'a most eccentric woman, her manner being decidedly peculiar.'

It wasn't the first time O'Hara had blurred the lines between his medical obligations and community expectations. And as Melbourne would soon find out, it wouldn't be the last.

CHAPTER 26

Mrs Howard stopped cold in the tiled corridor, her gloved fingers tightening around the handle of her purse.

She had travelled hundreds of miles from Sydney, stepped off the train at Spencer Street Station into the choking Melbourne heat, and criss-crossed the long, straight city blocks beneath the pitiless sun. She had waited outside Melbourne Gaol for hours, only to be turned away.

So instead, she had come to the Alfred Hospital, to the man her sister had shot. A man still injured. A man who was still, in some strange sense, part of the family.

There may have been more than duty in her visit. Perhaps, with the right tone, the right words, she could help calm the waters, smooth things over, lay the groundwork for reconciliation, or at least reduce the fallout to come.

She straightened her spine. Adjusted her hat. Took a step forward. A nurse moved to intercept her, beginning to speak, but it was already too late. From beyond the door came a clipped British voice: flat, cool, and final. 'I won't see her. She talks too much.'

Mrs Howard stood frozen, her pulse thudding in her ears. She turned without a word, skirts brushing the tiles as she walked away.

CHAPTER 27

As the press coverage rolled on throughout that first week, a strange thing was starting to happen. Mrs Fraser was becoming a star.

People saw in her whoever they wanted to see: an abused wife, a New Woman, a lunatic, a monster. From the dirty laneways of Richmond to the mansions of St Kilda, Melbourne was falling in love.

Newspapers such as the *Geelong Advertiser* had nothing but uncynical praise for her claimed talents. They showed no interest in verifying the details, only in amplifying them. Revelations of her athletic prowess, musicality and skill with firearms came thick and fast. *The Advertiser* gushed about how she could literally pepper a target with pistol bullets at long range, how she had swum vast distances in the open ocean, how she was both 'a vocalist of no mean order' and also 'an instrumentalist of considerable genius.'

The Advertiser did draw the line somewhere. Their enthusiasm didn't extend to her career as a mining speculator. Her success in mining investment, they implied, could be chalked up to luck. It was too much to suggest that this refined, beautiful, athletic superwoman might also possess a mind for investment. That, after all, was the province of men.

Part of Mrs Fraser's appeal was her enigmatic backstory in England. No one could quite pin her down. Some said that she had been a showgirl in a shooting gallery, others said she had been a ballerina, describing her as 'decidedly handsome and of somewhat stage-like appearance.'

One newspaper even claimed she was the daughter of an

Englishman of title, who had made a runaway match with Dr Fraser. A rival paper insisted her father was German, her mother Irish, and the family impoverished. Yet another source claimed she hailed from Jersey in the Channel Islands.

One specific story from her early life does survive, as relayed by Mrs Fraser herself to a reporter following the shooting. Whether fact, embellishment, or pure fantasy, it reveals a woman who understood the power of a compelling origin story. She claimed to have fled home before the age of sixteen, to escape a forced marriage to an elderly man of means. With just one shilling and ninepence to her name, she said she made her way to London and within days, secured a job in a firm employing six hundred staff. Six weeks later—still only sixteen—she was, by her own account, running the entire operation. They supposedly offered her seven pounds a week to stay. She declined. She had, she said, 'other plans.'

What the newspapers didn't report was that Melbourne had seen this woman before. Not in real life, but on the stage.

Some years earlier, Ibsen's *Hedda Gabler* had played to mixed reviews in Melbourne and across Australia. The eponymous heroine was described as a woman 'on the edge of reason, battling the world around her.' Beautiful, intelligent, restless, trapped in a life she couldn't abide. She manipulated other women, played dangerous games with men, and most strikingly, she sealed her fate with her father's pistols. The parallel was almost too perfect.

And like Mrs Fraser, audiences hadn't quite known what to make of her. Some saw Hedda as a tragic figure, a woman destroyed for refusing to conform. Others saw her as unnatural. Monstrous. Dangerous. One newspaper warned that the play undermined the institution of marriage itself.

The newspapers also failed to notice that Mrs Fraser had said something eerily familiar when travelling to the St Kilda Police Station in the hansom cab: 'Sometimes a sudden impulse comes over me, and I cannot resist it.' A line almost identical to Hedda Gabler's, just before her final descent.

And so, the legend was born. Mrs Fraser was Every Woman and No Woman. Singular yet generic. A mirror for a changing society's fantasies and its fears. Melbourne couldn't get enough.

CHAPTER 28

Beneath Melbourne's fascination with Mrs Fraser, something darker was simmering. As women stepped into new roles and pushed for greater rights, the backlash grew just as fiercely.

Late-Victorian society was gripped by gender anxiety: a dread that the Old Order was slipping, that the women who once stood by the hearth were now knocking on the doors of the boardroom, the courtroom, and even the parliament. When men felt that loss of control, they responded not with reason, but with ridicule.

The justice system was a microcosm of this struggle. Gender could be weaponised here, sometimes in a woman's favour, sometimes against her. A clever barrister could flip the script either way. If his client was a woman, he might lean into her supposed fragility, painting her as a delicate damsel who deserved sympathy. Purves had used that very tactic in the Phoebe Post trial, and again with Sealey and Fitzjames.

But if the woman was a witness for the Crown, that same barrister would pivot. Her womanhood would become a liability. Her sexual history, her hysteria, her shrewishness, her sharp tongue—everything was fair game. A woman became a caricature to be mocked into submission. And no one did it with more flair, or more cruelty, than James Liddell Purves QC.

One oft-recounted tale concerned a woman who refused to wilt. She planted her elbows on the edge of the witness box, leaned forward, and fixed Purves with a stare that said, *come on then. Let's see what you've got.*

Purves froze for a half-second, then saw an opportunity for

humour. He widened his eyes in mock alarm, and raised his hands in pantomime surrender. He took one step back, then another. Finally, with an exaggerated sigh, he sank heavily into his chair, as though struck by an invisible force, letting his body crumple in slow-motion defeat. The jury erupted.

Just a month before Mrs Fraser shot her husband, Finlayson had once again seen Purves demolish a female witness. It was a perjury trial, where a Mrs Hogan was Finlayson's star witness.

She had heard her son, the defendant, make various damning confessions about a fraud he was alleged to have perpetrated. But at trial, he had told a completely different story. So here they all were again, back in court for round two.

Mrs Hogan entered the witness box and was sworn in. Purves rose, the air thick with anticipation. He adjusted his silk robes, barely disguising his smirk. He surveyed the room like a gladiator in the Colosseum, knowing the crowd would soon be baying for blood.

Mrs Hogan had four marriages behind her. A fact that was irrelevant to the legal issues at hand, and equally irrelevant to her credibility as a witness. But for Purves, it was cross-examination gold.

He leaned forward, voice rich with exaggerated politeness. 'You have a very bad memory, haven't you? Well, we'll test it. Do you know how many husbands you've had?' Laughter ripped through the public gallery like flames from a match tossed into the dry Australian scrub. 'Do you find matrimony so…enjoyable?' he asked, with a tilt of mock curiosity.

'That is my own affair,' she snapped, chin high.

Purves spread his hands, his grin broadening. 'Oh, but I assure you, madam, it is now ours as well.'

Finlayson, the Crown's sentinel in his frayed old stuff wool gown, watched motionless as a reputable mother was reduced, moment by moment, into a joke. An embarrassment. A punchline.

Purves tarnished her reputation in every way he could imagine, flinging accusations like a butcher hurling offal into the gutter:

She got married only because she was pregnant.

She lied about her age on one of her marriage certificates.

She deserted one of her four husbands.

She felt no remorse when another one died.

She was a bigamist.

The Judge never intervened. Then came the coup de grâce:

'Did you marry Moore?' ... a dramatic pause ... 'I mean, *the man* Moore.' The public gallery groaned like half-cut punters at the Tivoli.

She cracked only once during the lengthy ordeal, retorting sharply, 'This is very funny of you Mr Purves, to make a woman look ridiculous and a fool in the witness box.'

In closing, he performed a little comedy routine. Purves asked the jury to imagine that Mrs Hogan was attending a séance to speak with her late husbands. He then acted the whole scene out, complete with hifalutin gestures and funny voices.

'Hullo Harrison, how are you getting on?' he sneered, mimicking Mrs Hogan with a high voice like a pantomime Dame.

'All riiiiight...' came the exaggerated other-worldly response, complete with mysterious hand gestures.

'Are you well and happy, Harrison?'

'Yessss.'

'Happier than when you were with me?'

'Yessss.' This ghostly line was delivered with particular emphasis.

'Where are you, Harrison?'

A loaded silence. Then—

'In hell.'

The jurymen rolled around the box in laughter.

The audacity didn't stop there.

Finlayson sat unblinking as Purves then asked the jury to find his client not guilty *without leaving the jury box*. This was irregular. The jury were meant to deliberate, to uphold the solemn duty of justice.

For a man like Finlayson, ritual-bound, creed-led, and steeped in the symbolism of higher orders, it would have felt as if the last rampart had fallen into the dust.

The jurymen exchanged glances. Brief, knowing. Then, as if moving in rehearsed unison, they turned to the judge and declared their verdict: 'Not guilty.' No deliberation. No hesitation.

And without leaving the jury box.

CHAPTER 29

Friday 6 October 1899

The St Kilda Police Court was heaving with onlookers. Every bench and inch of standing space was taken.

Ladies in lace-trimmed hats craned their necks, whispered behind gloved hands, and fanned away the rising heat. The air was thick with perfume, perspiration, and the unmistakable scent of scandal. Businessmen mixed with labourers at the back of the room. Journalists jostled for position.

Silence fell as the clerk announced the arrival of the magistrates. A full bench of eight entered, led by the fresh-faced Mayor A.V. Kemp. At just twenty-six years old, Kemp was Australia's youngest mayor. A real estate agent by profession, he was proud, alert, and visibly unaccustomed to this much public scrutiny.

The MAYOR OF ST. KILDA and Mrs. KEMP.

Mr. Kemp is the youngest Mayor in Australia, being only 26 years of age.

Kemp declared the proceedings open. McInerney glanced over at his client in the dock. She was clothed entirely in black. On her left hand, a wedding ring gleamed in defiance. A thick veil concealed her face, lending her the air of a woman caught between a royal funeral and a séance.

Representing the Crown was Inspector Crampton, a straight-as-a-die Police Prosecutor. As Crown Prosecutor, Finlayson wouldn't personally become involved until after Mrs Fraser's committal hearing.

Detective O'Donnell, perhaps still feeling bruised by McInerney's stunt with the second Dying Man's Deposition, sat next to Crampton. Only days earlier O'Donnell had taken to the newspapers, condemning McInerney's manoeuvre as an evidentiary farce.

McInerney looked around the packed courtroom, savouring the moment. The room hushed. He stood, straightening his back.

'Homeless, friendless, and alone,' McInerney declared, gesturing to the veiled figure in the dock. Journalists scribbled fervently, knowing they had just been handed tomorrow's headline. 'Your Worships,' he continued, voice rich with theatrical gravity, 'Mrs Fraser cannot, and will not, find a place in any hotel or coffee house in this city. Her case has become infamous, and no respectable establishment will take her in.'

He paused. The magistrates' eyes narrowed.

'But she has not been abandoned entirely,' McInerney continued, now softer, almost conspiratorial, 'The good sisters at Presentation Convent have graciously offered her sanctuary. A place of peace, where she may reside while awaiting trial. There, under their care, she will be watched over, kept away from the harsh gaze of the public, and no threat to anyone.'

The arrangement with the convent had been a masterstroke. It carried the air of penitence, restraint, and redemption. It would also ensure his client was under the eyes of women who would tolerate no further outbursts or erratic behaviour. The irony was hard to miss. A convent. A black veil. All for a woman who had shouted 'I did it!' while standing over a smoking revolver. One can imagine McInerney turning away from the bench, dabbing at his brow under pretence of needing his handkerchief, jaw clenched to suppress the laugh rising unbidden in his chest.

'She is a woman who has suffered much,' he went on, placing just enough emotion in his voice. 'And in these difficult times, the sanctuary of the convent is not just a refuge. It is a necessity.'

'If she were not to be allowed bail,' continued McInerney, 'she might be confined in gaol for months, for if her husband does recover, his convalescence would be slow. This is a woman, a wife, with no criminal history. To keep her in custody would be an absurdity, Your Worships. I ask for bail in two sureties of two hundred pounds each, and a surety from Mrs Fraser in the sum of one thousand pounds.' He sat down.

'Mr Crampton?' asked Mayor Kemp.

Crampton rose, his voice sharp and direct. He reminded the bench that Mrs Fraser was charged with one of the most serious offences in the law—attempted murder—a capital crime that, upon conviction, carried the penalty of death. In such circumstances, he argued, the risk of absconding couldn't be ignored. Mrs Fraser, he noted, was both wealthy and well-travelled. She had the means and motivation to flee the jurisdiction. Granting bail in such a case, he warned, would be reckless.

One of the magistrates, Mr Stedeford, piped up. 'There was a death in Dr Gaze's case, yet he was admitted to bail.'

McInerney leapt to his feet, seizing this gift like a hungry dog grabbing a steak off the table. 'Yes, your Worship, that is correct. That is the reason we seek the sureties I have proposed. They were identical in the Gaze matter.'

Dr William Henry Gaze had been one of the defendants in the infamous Boot Box Murder, a sensational trial heard by the Victorian Supreme Court earlier that year.

The Boot Box Murder had sent shockwaves through Melbourne. Mabel Ambrose, just seventeen, had died following a crude abortion attempt. Her body was stuffed into a boot box and dumped in the Yarra. McInerney had served on the defence team representing Dr William Henry Gaze, one of the accused.

At the mention of the Boot Box Murder, O'Donnell likely bristled. He had worked that investigation too. The cold stillness of the morgue, watching as the girl's decaying body was laid out, was burned on his brain. And how her head was then surgically removed from her body and paraded around Melbourne like some gruesome sideshow attraction, in the desperate hope that someone might identify her.

Crampton rose once more. He reminded the magistrates that while the charge was grave, the surrounding circumstances made the matter even more serious. Mrs Fraser had, by her own admission, discharged a revolver during what appeared to be a fit of emotional distress. Her physical fragility, he suggested, must be weighed against the evident volatility of her actions. The safety of the public, he concluded, had to remain the paramount concern.

'Does the inspector really want to keep this woman, who is innocent until proven guilty, in gaol for two or three months before her trial?' McInerney shot back, with a raised voice.

Yet again, Stedeford tossed McInerney a bone, and this one had marrow. He was starting to look less like an impartial judge and more like a silent partner in McInerney and McInerney.

'This case is such a conflicting one, and there is such a difference of opinion, that it is not likely to come on for six months,' he drawled.

McInerney leaned forward, already halfway out of his chair, primed to lavish praise on the JP for his excellent observation. But Crampton cut him off.

'The responsibility is with Your Worships. I have done my duty,' he said.

The bench conferred in low tones, eyes down, heads tilted.

The courtroom held its breath, the hush deepening like the air before a storm.

CHAPTER 30

'Bail will be granted,' the baby-faced Mayor Kemp pronounced, his voice slow and deliberate. 'Two sureties of five hundred pounds each, and Mrs Fraser herself in for one thousand pounds.' The sound of the gavel hitting the bench echoed like the first cannon shot before a battle.

The names of her sureties caused something of a stir. One was Mr A.W. Ferne, the proprietor of London & American Stores, a vertically integrated textile empire with factories and retail outlets across Melbourne and Sydney. The other was Mr King O'Malley.

Flamboyant, theatrical, and famously unbothered by the constraints of fact, O'Malley was a progressive South Australian politician. Conservatives mocked him as much for his flowing capes and exotic backstory as they did for his support of women's rights. Hailing from the United States, he claimed to have been raised by Native American Indians. Then came the yarn about his arrival in Australia: crawling into a cave on death's door with tuberculosis, he was saved—he insisted—by a mystic Aboriginal healer.

As much of a walking headline as he was a politician, O'Malley had once again inserted himself into the middle of a story. This was just the kind of cause that suited him: a distressed woman, a legal system stacked against her, and enough scandal to keep both of their names in the press for months to come.

It was reported that Mrs Fraser had known neither Ferne nor O'Malley before the shooting incident. She had written to them from her prison cell.

While O'Donnell and the court officials processed the bail paperwork, McInerney and Mrs Fraser waited in the anteroom. Inspector Crampton hovered nearby, as did at least one journalist.

Still veiled, Mrs Fraser turned to McInerney with a flashing smile. 'It will all come right in the end.' she exclaimed. Her bright voice filled the room; Crampton couldn't help but overhear. McInerney looked on, wary. This was a dangerous game.

'He will recover,' she continued, her eyes gleaming beneath the veil, 'and he will tell the whole story. When that happens, it will show that I had no intention to shoot him—no, no—it was a sudden impulse, a rash act, when he accused me of infidelity. The jury will understand, don't you think? They'll do me justice, I'm sure they will.'

McInerney's eyes narrowed. This was too loud. Too explicit. Too close to the police, and the press. She was speaking of temper, of impulse, of provocation. But that was not her defence. Her defence was insanity. Words like these could sink her before she even faced a jury.

'You see,' she continued, her words spilling like water from a broken dam, 'Dr Fraser has admitted that I have had a revolver for a long time, and that it was he who taught me to shoot. Why, we practised in Tasmania with revolvers and rifles until I became expert with both. I could shoot left-handed or right-handed with a revolver, and with a rifle I was a dead shot at a reasonable distance, and could give good account of myself on a rifle range at a thousand yards.' She gave a strange tinkling laugh. One that was far too loud for the room.

One could imagine McInerney's hand darting towards her arm, or his index finger rising to his lips in a silent plea.

Oblivious to her lawyer's concerns, she beckoned Crampton over. He walked towards her, mesmerised. Her eyes caught his and held them, unblinking, with a smile just wide enough to blur the line between charm and mischief.

In full control of the room, she now held up a tiny scrap of newspaper. 'See this piece of paper?' she asked, her amplified voice the call of a showgirl at a country fair. 'Well, the doctor would hold a bit of wood this size in his fingers, and I would crash it with a revolver bullet from a dozen yards. That was quite a common bit of entertainment for us.'

'But was it not dangerous?' Crampton asked with a raised eyebrow.

'Yes, perhaps,' she replied, her voice ringing out with a rustic cadence that was almost musical. 'Of course, it would have been unpleasant for the doctor if I had been a bad or nervous shot. But you see,' she added with a wink, 'I was not.'

A bead of sweat might by now have formed on McInerney's temple, a silent scream that begged her to stop before it was too late. But his client was already clearing her throat and turning back to her audience.

With her attention now entirely on Crampton, she tilted her head and regaled the incredulous Inspector with tales of her former life in Tasmania. The guns, the hunting, the bicycle rides. How she had ridden her husband's bicycle dressed in men's clothes. How she could ride a spirited mare bareback with ease. How, when shooting wild fowl, she always took the birds on the wing. 'Like all sportsmen,' she confided with a knowing smile, 'I would have scorned to shoot them sitting.'

McInerney breathed a sigh of relief when O'Donnell interrupted. The paperwork was going to be delayed, he told them, requiring a return trip to Melbourne Gaol.

Waiting for his client to be released from gaol later that day, McInerney perhaps allowed himself a moment of self-congratulation, a small pat on the back for a job well done. He had secured her release in challenging circumstances. Now, she would be placed in the care of the Presentation Sisters, where she would be kept out of trouble and shielded from public scrutiny.

Or so McInerney believed. O'Donnell later claimed in his memoirs that Mrs Fraser never went to the Presentation Convent at all, but instead went straight from gaol to the house of a friend—likely Mrs McCormick of Mary Street, St Kilda—where she stayed.

Kathleen Fraser had won her freedom.

But the game, it seemed, had only just begun.

CHAPTER 31

Following Mrs Fraser's release on bail, an odd little item appeared in *The Herald*. Not about firearms, marital quarrels, or insanity—but about a wedding ring.

In court, the gold band on her finger hadn't gone unnoticed. *The Herald* reported that it had been taken from her by Melbourne Gaol when she was first incarcerated, and returned on the morning of her bail hearing. But now, at the gaol Governor's insistence, *The Herald* was issuing a correction.

'It is not true,' the Governor wrote, 'that the ring had been taken from her by the authorities and then returned.' On the contrary, he insisted, Mrs Fraser didn't have a wedding ring when she was admitted to gaol. Nor was one ever returned to her by the warders. The Governor wanted to make the position clear: Melbourne Gaol would never deprive any woman accused of a crime of her wedding ring.

Which meant, of course, that Mrs Fraser wasn't wearing a wedding ring when she left Melbourne Gaol. And yet, by the time she entered the dock, one had miraculously appeared on her finger.

One might imagine Finlayson's reaction as he read this article over morning tea at the Crown Law Offices.

A widow's veil. A black dress. A band of gold. They were small details, but telling.

The ring was no accident.

It was a prop.

Crown Law Offices, Lonsdale Street — Nettleton and Arnest
Museums Victoria Collection

CHAPTER 32

In late 1899, itinerant sewerage labourer John Foster returned to Melbourne from Sydney. Like a moth to the flame, he couldn't stay away from his on-again, off-again lover Amy Alice Peterson. She had bewitched him, and he had to find her. To possess her.

Foster was a rough-hewn manual worker, with a scar on his forehead and half the middle finger of his left hand missing. A Jekyll and Hyde character, he was quiet and inoffensive when sober, but had a violent temper when drunk.

His relationship with Peterson, a sometime domestic servant and occasional fruit hawker, was as volatile and poisonous as that of the warring Frasers, but with one important difference. The Frasers were members of Melbourne's elite; Foster and Peterson belonged to the dregs. If the Frasers' relationship was a melodrama performed in the parlours of high society, Foster and Peterson's was a sordid street brawl.

Class differences aside, *The Bendigo Advertiser* could easily have been describing the Frasers when it lamented the situation of Foster and Peterson as 'One of those unfortunate and miserable...relations often formed between men and women, in which incompatibility of temperament leads to ready separation, and unbridled passions are given full play.'

Their existence was a perpetual scrabble on the margins, their pockets empty and their lives unobserved by the watchful eyes of propriety.

That is, until he tried to kill her.

John Foster

CHAPTER 33

4 November 1899

'Fifty pounds, Paul. That's all I need.'

Mrs Fraser stood near her husband's bed, eyes flashing. Her voice, loud and urgent, cut through the scented air like a knife through damask.

Dr Fraser lay propped against the pillows, face pale, left eye swathed in bandages. He shifted slightly, as though her mere presence caused him discomfort. When he spoke, his voice was firm but weary.

'No.'

She stiffened. 'I need that money. To furnish the terrace. Our home.'

'I won't give it to you.'

John Robins, the orderly assigned to Dr Fraser, had witnessed plenty of uneasy visits between patients and their spouses, but nothing quite like this.

Mrs Evans' Private Hospital, nestled in a genteel corner of St Kilda, was known for its calm and discretion. Dr Fraser had transferred there to escape the noise and chaos of the Alfred. But that morning, tranquillity had given way to turmoil.

Robins padded around the room, straightening linen, checking supplies, all the while doing his best to ignore the growing tension.

Mrs Fraser's voice grew louder. 'Come to Mary Street and live with me. I can care for you better there.'

He refused again, and she snapped.

Curse words flew—*cad*, *cur*, and worse. Robins, flushed at the language, fussed with the sterilised gauze tins on the shelf.

She stepped closer to the bed, hissing 'You are my husband!'

He sat mute, refusing to meet her gaze.

Then came the change.

The tilt of her head. The sudden stillness.

Her voice dropped to a whisper.

'I wish to God I had finished you when I was at it.'

She let out a tight breath, spun on her heel, and stormed from the room.

Her husband let out a long, uneven breath, his body sinking into the pillows. He looked at Robins.

'Did you hear that?'

Robins nodded.

He had heard every word.

CHAPTER 34

9 December 1899 - Howard Street, North Melbourne

John Foster paced the alley, the stench of rotting hides from the tanneries thick in his throat. Sweat trickled down his spine, soaked into his collar, but he barely noticed. His mind was boiling.

Howard Street swam before him, the air shimmering, the bluestones slick with heat. The door of number twenty-six loomed ahead; peeling and cracked, warped by sun and time. He clenched his fists, knuckles white.

He knocked. The door trembled.

A pause, then the slow scrape of a latch. Alice.

She didn't step forward. Didn't invite him in.

Behind her, a small girl peeked out from the folds of her skirt. She was barefoot, thin arms clutching a rag doll.

The exchange between them was brief. Quiet. A few short phrases, low and tense. From the street, no one heard what was said. But whatever words were offered—an apology, a promise, a plea—they didn't land. The door slammed shut.

Silence.

His breath came fast, ragged. His skin burned, his head throbbed. The whole street was too bright, too sharp. His boots moved on their own, carrying him inexorably forward. They knew what he had to do.

***

Victoria Street, North Melbourne. Thirty minutes later.

The bell above the door of Mrs Fyfe's ironmonger's shop jangled.

Foster drifted inside.

A row of butchers' knives gleamed in the window, their edges catching the light like cruel smiles. One of them shimmered with a strange clarity, like it had been waiting to be chosen.

His fingers twitched. Hovered. Wrapped around cool steel. The weight of it was solid. Steady. A breath shuddered from his lungs. This was what he needed.

CHAPTER 35

Mrs Fraser was back at her husband's bedside.

Like a stuck gramophone record, the couple replayed the same dialogue from her last visit, whilst Robins hovered in the background. She implored her husband to leave the hospital and come live with her. He refused, firm and unmoved.

At last, Robins stepped forward. Drawing himself to full height, he moved between them and asked her to leave.

For a beat, she stood motionless. Robins braced for the storm.

But then, just like that, she obeyed. As she swept past him, Robins allowed himself a small smile of satisfaction. This time, it had been easy. No screaming, and no threats. He escorted her out of the front door and through the front garden to the gate. He kept close, but not too close. He'd got the measure of her ... steady, firm, don't engage. Guide, don't force. No need for the police. No need for—

She ducked.

A blur of motion. A flicker of fabric. She turned on a sixpence, slipped past him, and raced back to her husband's room.

Robins sprinted after her. By the time he got there, she was already bent over the bed, hands quivering and blonde curls bouncing in all directions. Her face twisted with something raw, something dark. Her husband shrank back against the pillows.

She glared at him like a modern-day Medea, the very archetype of a woman scorned.

Then, bending closer, she flung the words like a curse—words that sent a shudder crawling down Robins' spine.

'Then I shall do for the child.'

CHAPTER 36

Back at twenty-six Howard Street, Foster slammed his fist against the front door. Locked. He rattled the knob, then shoved his shoulder against the wood. Harder. Harder. The frame groaned but held.

He stalked down the side of the house and round to the high back fence, sweat now slick on his back. Without breaking stride, he leapt, hauling himself up, boots scraping, muscles burning. He swung over, landing crouched in the yard.

The back door was also locked.

With a howl, he hurled himself against it. Wood splintered, the frame shuddering. Again. Again. Breath tore from his lungs in ragged bursts. One last savage slam and the door burst inward.

He staggered into the gloom.

A rustle. A footstep. Running.

His pulse spiked. He lunged down the hall. Ahead, a warped sheet of glass shimmered in an internal door. Beyond was Alice, her arms wrapped tight around her little girl, clutching her so close she could barely move.

For a moment, they stared at each other.

Then she bolted.

He surged forward.

Glass exploded. A deafening crack, like a gunshot. The door shattered around him. Shards flew. His coat tore, his skin sliced, his face bled. He didn't stop. Didn't feel it.

Alice shrieked and scrambled for the front door. The child cried. Foster stepped through the wreckage, glass crunching under his boots like broken bone.

They made it outside. Sunlight. Street. People.

But then—a stumble. The child's foot caught on the hem of her dress. She tottered.

Alice halted, just a flicker of hesitation.

He closed the gap in two strides. His fist knotted in her dress, yanking hard.

She spun, breathless, wild-eyed. 'John—please!'

He didn't hear. The knife flashed.

She raised her arm. A sharp, wet slice. She gasped, blood spilling down her sleeve.

Another blow. He aimed for the heart. The blade hit something solid—a brooch. It glanced off with a hollow clang.

'Help! Police!' Her voice shrieked through the thick air. Her hands clawed at him, nails dragging down his skin, but he barely felt it.

He grinned, breath hot, eyes wild. He raised the knife high. This time—this time—

The blade came down.

CHAPTER 37

Mid-swing, Foster felt his arm wrenched back with brutal force.

He twisted around, snarling, eyes blazing with fury as he faced the policeman who had seized him.

Constable John Lochram wrestled with Foster's wrists, his grip iron-tight despite the man's thrashing strength. Alice fled down the street behind them, clutching the child to her chest.

Lochram shouted to a passerby. 'Take the knife! Now, quickly!'

The man, a local labourer, stepped forward. Foster dropped the blade before he even got close. The metal hit the baking bluestones with a sharp clang, spinning for a moment before lying still.

Foster's lips twisted into a chilling smile, his voice almost triumphant as he declared, 'I'm satisfied now. I've done what I intended to do.'

The labourer patted Foster down under Lochram's direction, his expression turning to horror as he withdrew two long black cases from Foster's coat. The lids clicked open, revealing the gleaming blades of two cutthroat razors, each one sharp enough to slice through leather.

Constable Davey arrived, red-faced and panting. He'd heard the screaming from two streets over.

Together, the constables hauled Foster to his feet. He offered no resistance. 'I'm very sorry I never finished that bloody woman.' he mused, his tone disturbingly conversational. 'Look here, old man. If you only knew the injury that woman has done to me, you wouldn't blame me for what I've done.'

At the watchhouse, they went through every pocket and fold of Foster's coat. Davey reached inside and froze.

His fingers had found the cold metal of a fully loaded revolver.

CHAPTER 38

9 December 1899

Senior Constable George Doran Williams wished he'd seen the last of Mrs Fraser the day he dispatched her to Melbourne Gaol back in September. But like a rogue comet, she kept dragging him back into her orbit.

This time, he was waiting just inside the locked front door of Mrs Evans' Private Hospital. Behind him stood Mrs Evans and John Robins, stiff with anxiety. Even through the thick oak door, he could hear Mrs Fraser pacing outside, her footsteps crisp on the gravel.

Williams exhaled. Enough was enough.

He raised his voice. Calm. Firm. Authoritative. Told her to leave —now.

A pause. Then, footsteps, retreating up the path.

Williams turned to the others with a small nod. That should do it. A few stern words from a copper. She was out on bail, after all. She couldn't afford fresh trouble. He reached for the door handle.

But there was no click of the gate. The footsteps were now making their way through the garden. Williams peered through the lace curtains and saw her walk towards her husband's window on the ground floor.

She reached the window and stopped. Her voice, sharp as cut glass, echoed off the walls: 'If you don't see me, I'll make it hot for you. I'll get you ten years! I'll get a divorce!'

No response.

Then she shouted something stranger still. 'I didn't shoot

you. You know I'm shielding you, but I won't do so any longer!'

Williams threw the door open and strode outside, boots crunching on the gravel. Mrs Fraser spun toward him, flushed and breathy.

Without a word, he took her by the arm and led her from the premises.

Inside, Dr Fraser had already rung his bell.

'Robins,' he said, voice low and tight, 'Call Mr Corr.'

CHAPTER 39

Finlayson had never seen a trial taken less seriously.

The jurymen were leaning back in their chairs, laughing like it was a Christmas pantomime. The barristers, some of the highest profile in Melbourne, were chuckling amongst themselves. Even the judge, his Honour Justice Thomas A'Beckett, had to wipe an occasional tear of laughter from his eye.

This time, Finlayson was here as a witness. He had been called to give evidence in a defamation trial about things said in court when he prosecuted accountant Joseph Flanagan for fraud earlier that year. The original fraud case had been a sensation, with the defendant spilling scandalous allegations against his accuser, prominent businessman Andrew Rowan, like sly grog in a backroom bar. Flanagan, a detail-focussed numbers man, had even printed a pamphlet in which Rowan's dubious transactions were recounted in painstaking detail, calculated down to the last pound, shilling and penny.

Purves had acted for Flanagan, who, predictably, had walked free.

Now, this trial—*Charles Johnston v. the Argus*—was a surreal aftershock.

In one of his long, looping orations in the original fraud trial, Purves had allegedly said that Mr Charles Johnson, a clerk employed by Andrew Rowan, had also engaged in fraudulent activity. Such words, if said, were ruinous to the man's reputation. In their coverage of the trial, Purves' longstanding client *The Argus* had published those words without first checking the facts. So now, Charles Johnston was suing them for libel.

The irony? Purves should have been the star witness, not sitting at the bar table. But somehow, he had manipulated his way into representing *The Argus*. A walking conflict of interest, he strutted around the courtroom like it was his own personal fiefdom.

The Victorian Bar had rules about these things, or so they claimed. The Committee of Counsel's own rules of etiquette made it clear: *a barrister shall be careful not to place himself in a position which might expose him to suspicion that his private interests conflict with his professional duty.*

Yet this was a set up so bent you could use it as a coat hook. If Purves admitted he'd said the alleged words, *The Argus* was safe as they would have accurately reported what was said in open court. But if he backpedalled, fudged, or claimed he'd named someone else, then his good client was liable for defamation.

And yet, A'Beckett let Purves run the defence.

Why?

Because Purves was one of them. And Melbourne's wealthy elite looked after their own.

Finlayson could surely see it now, the truth that had likely been gnawing at him for years. Purves wasn't the problem. The problem was the system that let him do whatever he pleased.

A lowly Amalgam would have been thrown out of court for pulling a stunt like this. But Purves? He was too entrenched, too connected.

Justice Hamilton, the original trial judge, took the stand. His cross-examination was a joke. None of the barristers went anywhere near a difficult question. The whole thing had the easy rhythm of a club lunch. Hamilton played along. When asked whether lawyers ever made mistakes, Hamilton gestured to the young barrister cross-examining him. With the polish of a music hall comedian, and perhaps a sly wink, he quipped, 'They are invariably making mistakes *like this!*' The courtroom howled. Even the jury chuckled along.

Melbourne liked to think of itself as modern, progressive, better than the old country. But the Victorian Bar? To Finlayson, it must at times have felt like a throwback to his formative years as a pupil barrister in London. Back then doorkeepers hawked trials like sideshows, barristers trained with stage actors, and the crowd booed witnesses like pantomime villains. Looking around the courtroom now, it seemed that little had changed.

Finlayson was sworn in. He had rehearsed his words, ready to state the facts with care and clarity. But when he took the stand, even he couldn't resist being dragged into the circus.

When asked whether Purves had given a long or short speech in the original trial, Finlayson quipped, 'For Purves, it was about medium.' Laughter rippled. Even Purves grinned. Finlayson likely felt cheap the moment he said it. He might have gotten a laugh, but he'd just tacitly condoned their shenanigans.

Pulling himself together, Finlayson gave his evidence with candour, making concessions as required. Most of that evidence favoured his nemesis Purves, but he put it forward without fear or favour. He was under oath, and it was the right thing to do.

The final verdict? A pyrrhic victory for the plaintiff, Charles Johnston. The jury found that *The Argus* had indeed defamed him, and awarded nominal damages of one farthing.

But from a commercial perspective, it was a big loss for Purves and his client. Despite Purves' protests, the judge ruled that the newspaper would have to pay the plaintiff's legal costs.

In his life, Charles Braine Finlayson didn't often speak of principle. He preferred to live by it. But when he did give voice to his convictions, it was usually within the closed walls of the Masonic Lodge among brethren and ritual, in the language of symbols, oaths, and duty.

Like many professional men of his time, Finlayson was active in freemasonry. Back in 1874, he had been appointed Worshipful Master of the Yarrowee Lodge. In his acceptance speech, Finlayson spoke of the day he would pass on the role to his successor, handing back his badge of office, 'as pure and unsullied' as he received it.

To him, these were more than ceremonial words. They became a kind of private creed: to serve with honour, and to guard what was entrusted to him as custodian for his successor.

And as he left the courtroom that day, Finlayson might quietly have renewed that same solemn vow.

CHAPTER 40

Following Mrs Fraser's release on bail, McInerney continued to represent her tirelessly through to Christmas of 1899. He appeared at all her subsequent bail applications, one every three or four weeks, each time keeping her out of gaol.

At one such appearance, he was pleased to inform the bench that Dr Fraser's recovery had reached near-miraculous levels. His left eye, which was previously thought lost, was now said to be 'completely restored.' The magistrates granted bail for a further month, but McInerney couldn't help himself. With Dr Fraser recovering, and his wife now by his side nursing him back to health, McInerney suggested the proceedings might be dropped altogether.

Inspector Crampton's response, 'Oh, that is nonsense!' was met with laughter from the packed courtroom.

McInerney also facilitated a tender reunion at Mrs Evans' hospital between Dr Fraser and Katie, the young daughter he shared with Mrs Fraser. No one, it seemed, was troubled by the ethics of the defendant's lawyer fraternising with the victim in this cosy manner.

Yet sometime before Christmas, McInerney ceased acting for Mrs Fraser. The reasons remain unknown.

He had served her well, securing her release on bail and successfully arguing each and every renewal. And although his second Dying Man's Deposition was ultimately unsuccessful, the strategy had been brilliant and daring.

Perhaps he felt disrespected, even ethically compromised, after Mrs Fraser sabotaged his plan for her to enter the Presentation Convent.

Alternatively, Mrs Fraser may have terminated the retainer, seeking more prominent representation. With her life on the line, and money no object, she may have gone looking for a high profile QC.

But even that might not explain it, because McInerney knew when to step back. In the Boot Box Murder trial, he had briefed a high-profile barrister without hesitation. Had Mrs Fraser asked him to instruct a QC to represent her in Court, with McInerney to assume the traditional solicitor's role, it's likely he would have agreed.

What is known is that a new solicitor came onto the record in late 1899 or early 1900: Mr Henry Hale Budd.

Hale Budd then promptly briefed his cousin, James Liddell Purves QC.

When the curtain rose in the new year, Mrs Fraser would have a new leading man.

CHAPTER 41

In individuals, insanity is rare; but in groups, parties, nations, and epochs, it is the rule.

— Friedrich Nietzsche, *Beyond Good and Evil*, 1886

Even as he fought Mrs Fraser's battles in court, McInerney's thoughts were increasingly elsewhere.

His younger brother and business partner Tim was preparing to leave for South Africa. A long-time army reservist, Lieutenant Tim McInerney found himself at the top of the list. Others were not so lucky. In her first imperial war, Australia had resolved to send only her best and strongest to support the motherland. Military doctors rejected scores of men who weren't fit enough. Women who volunteered as nurses were turned away in droves. Men who could shoot straight and passed the fitness tests were still excluded if they didn't possess a *military gait* in the saddle. Volunteers who questioned the motives of Empire — or worse, mentioned diamonds — were quietly shown the door.

Soon, the Bendigo Advertiser was hailing Tim as the city's favourite son, a 'remarkably fine specimen of young Victoria.' He would, they reported, have received his captain's commission that very month had he remained in Australia; instead, he volunteered to go as a mere lieutenant, which only burnished his credentials. The ladies of Melbourne were delighted to learn he was unmarried.

On 28 October, McInerney attended the grand military procession farewelling the first Victorian contingent. He draped himself in three flags for the occasion: the Union Jack, the Irish Tricolour, and the new Australian flag.

Cries of 'Godspeed, lads!' and 'Bring back glory!' rang out with the beat of drums and the bright notes of brass. Handkerchiefs waved; gloved hands rose in salute. In deference to those behind them, women wore compact gem hats. Men clambered onto verandas and lamp posts to snatch a view above crowds six deep. As Lieutenant Tim marched past the law offices of McInerney & McInerney, staff leaned from the windows and cheered him on.

First Australian Contingent marches down Bourke Street

It is not known whether Mrs Fraser met McInerney's gallant younger brother, nor whether she attended the parade that day. But as Melbourne would soon learn, she was paying close attention. If war could elevate a dashing lieutenant to hero status, why couldn't it do the same for a feisty young woman?

For McInerney, the day was bittersweet. With his brother gone, he would now shoulder the full weight of their busy practice alone, all while eyeing a run for the Victorian Parliament the following year. And Tim's departure left more than work to carry. The brothers had lived a sociable bachelor life at the home they shared in Carlton. They were known to set a table for four each evening, with an ever-changing parade of clients, politicians, and notables dropping in. But now, their dining room housed a Round Table without its knight.

From *the Argus*, 30 October 1899

CHAPTER 42

After more than three decades at the Bar, in late 1899 Charles Braine Finlayson finally yielded.

His old stuff wool gown, the junior barrister's robe he had likely purchased in London in the 1860s, was now threadbare. The hems were frayed, the seams worn smooth by decades of service. It had become a standing joke of the Melbourne Bar.

Some said the shabby gown marked him as a modest man, almost monk-like. But there was another interpretation: a trace of hidden pride. So long as he wore that same old gown, he hadn't yet given up hope of being appointed Queen's Counsel and swapping it for shiny new silk. To buy a new stuff wool gown would be to admit defeat, signalling to himself and the world that he would end his long career as a junior barrister.

But in the end, Finlayson couldn't ignore the growing wear and tear. Nor the mockery of his colleagues. At last, he capitulated. He ordered a new stuff wool gown that he would wear to the end.

Or so he thought.

CHAPTER 43

Melbourne was already brimming with scandals. But in the lead-up to Christmas, a new one erupted.

The city's Catholic faithful had packed into the newly consecrated Sacred Heart Church in Carlton to hear Archbishop Thomas Carr deliver the inaugural sermon. The occasion was solemn, the music soaring. From the choir loft Dr Henry O'Hara sang *Ave Maria*, his rich baritone rising like incense through the arches, reverent and aching with devotion.

But when Carr started preaching, the mood shifted.

Carr warned of a grave new moral threat to the city: a syndicate of prominent Melbourne citizens were attempting to commercialise a product that would, in his words, 'defeat the primary end of marriage and systematise one of the gravest violations of the moral law.' In other words, a contraceptive. Few in the congregation understood what he meant. Within days, the newspapers made it all too clear.

Archbishop Thomas Carr

At the centre of the scandal was Silenette Proprietary Limited, a new company which had developed and was marketing a chemical birth control product.

The Argus got the scoop, securing an exclusive interview with Carr. 'It is the most disgraceful thing that ever occurred in Melbourne,' the Archbishop declared, a bold claim about a city where the dispossession and genocide of its indigenous peoples was still within living memory.

The Women's Christian Temperance Movement agreed with Carr. Their Superintendent for Purity issued her own pronouncement: 'The deliberate avoidance of motherhood is the degradation of womanhood.'

The Advocate struck next, delivering a blow no one saw coming.

They revealed that the inventor behind Silenette—the man who had sold his secret formula in exchange for a substantial shareholding—was none other than Dr Henry O'Hara himself.

1899 advertisement for Silenette

CHAPTER 44

Barely a week after buying his new stuff wool gown, everything changed for Charles Braine Finlayson.

On the recommendation of the Chief Justice, and in recognition of his decades of quiet excellence, he was appointed Queen's Counsel by the Executive Counsel of the Victorian Government.

The newspapers couldn't resist the irony: just days after buying that new stuff wool gown, he now had another gown to order, this time in shimmering, embroidered silk.

The Victorian Supreme Court closed for the Christmas break on Friday, 22 December 1899. Sir John Madden, the Chief Justice and Henry O'Hara's cousin, remained in Melbourne to handle the vacation work, allowing his brother judges to retreat to their summer residences. Justice A'Beckett travelled to Portsea, Melbourne's answer to the Hamptons. Justices Hodges and Hood withdrew to their respective sprawling homes at Mount Macedon, escaping the city heat in Victoria's most exclusive highland retreat.

That Christmas, James Liddell Purves QC played honorary auctioneer at the Princess Theatre, selling seats for a benefit performance in aid of the Theatrical Charities Fund.

But true to form, it was his own performance that stole the spotlight. *Stella's Ladies' Letter* in *Table Talk* gushed 'The learned QC certainly gave them all the entertainment they desired, for he was in his best humorous vein'.

When bidding opened for the coveted proscenium boxes, the most expensive seats in the house, Purves spotted three attractive women seated in one of them. He couldn't help himself. He gestured toward the box, letting his gaze linger—just a little too long.

'Now there's a box,' he declared, 'the merits of which I need not dilate on.'

The crowd laughed.

'You know what it's worth,' he went on. 'Why, at present, I wouldn't mind giving forty thousand for it myself.'

Stella's Ladies' Letter reported that 'the three fair occupants blushed becomingly,' to thunderous applause.

The columnist then added, with a wink, that Purves 'never showed rudeness to a lady in the witness box greater than the politeness he showed to the ladies in the boxes of the stage.'

Later that evening, he proved his chivalry again, publicly scolding a male bidder for outbidding the only woman to raise her hand. 'Shockingly ungallant!' he declared.

Purves' charm, wit, and relentless coaxing helped raise a staggering £475 for the cause.

Finlayson worked right up until Christmas. Showing that no case was beneath him even after taking silk, he prosecuted a theft case involving a boy who took a cow from a neighbouring paddock. He secured a guilty verdict; then spent a quiet Christmas at the Camberwell home he shared with his two unmarried sisters.

For Mrs Fraser, the season of goodwill presented an opportunity to re-ingratiate herself with her husband, through sending gifts. On 21 December she sent their daughter with gifts of a pipe, a pouch full of tobacco, cigarettes, some scent, and a card wishing him the compliments of the season. On 30 December, a tobacco box, ash tray, light holder, and a box containing three bottles of scent. Then, on 14 January, two sets of pyjamas.

Dr Fraser accepted all the gifts, although he later testified that he never wore the pyjamas.

McInerney attended the Williamstown Grammar School Christmas concert in his official capacity for Melbourne University. He gave a rousing speech, presenting a silver-mounted walking stick to the school's Principal.

McInerney's brother Tim, already promoted to acting captain, spent Christmas on the front line in South Africa. In a letter home, he bemoaned his army rations of dry bread and water, with an occasional drop of tea and lump of meat. He complained that the Australian soldiers were worked harder than their British counterparts, and that he had already lost two stones in weight. On the positive side, he reported that he had grown 'as hard as nails.'

Corr attended the final 1899 meeting of the Prahran branch of the Australian Natives Association, where he took part in a debate on women's suffrage against the Prahran Presbyterian Literary Society. Corr invoked scripture, arguing that if the colony were to grant the vote to women, it would take them out of the sphere allotted to them by God himself, being the home. He concluded by clarifying that the low turnout of men to vote in elections was also, in fact, the fault of women. 'How is it that so many men do not exercise their votes?' he thundered from the stage, before answering his own question. 'Because women, instead of attending to their duties, are gadding about, and not training their boys to vote as they should.'

In response Miss Ackman of the Prahran Presbyterian Literary Society took a class-related approach. 'The privilege of voting no longer belongs to the cultured,' she explained, 'but is exercised by the labourer, the coal-heaver, and the chimney sweeper...The spirit of the age is to give citizenship to all, and it is not right to refuse the women what is granted to the most ignorant man.'

When the meeting voted, Corr and his colleagues from the A.N.A. were declared the winners.

O'Donnell's caseload over the festive season included investigating an obstruction on a suburban railway line. The trail led to a chubby four-year-old boy, who confessed without hesitation. O'Donnell delivered him to the custody of his parents.

Christmas day was blistering hot. 'It is a defiance of fate' one columnist observed, 'to sit down before a gargantuan goose, ponderous puddings and leviathan mince pies, with the thermometer 100 deg. in the shade; but the Briton, or the descendant of that robust Imperialist, does so without a scruple, and enjoys his fare just the same as if he were in bleak Inverness or trying to penetrate the obscurity of a London fog.'

On New Year's Eve, Melburnians gathered at the East Melbourne Cricket Ground for a lavish display of fireworks. The highlight was a reenactment of the recent battle at Modder Bridge. Fireworks mimicked the moment of the bridge's explosion —an exhilarating tribute to the might of the British Empire against the cowardly Boers. At the finale, a series of cannon-like booms rolled out, and fire streaked through the night. The spectacle was so vivid that some in the crowd gasped and clutched each other's arms. A military band played, and afterwards the scent of gunpowder lingered in the air, completing the illusion of an actual battlefield with sight, sound, and now even smell engaged in the celebration of Empire.

As Melbourne's festive season ended, one of its final events went unnoticed by the city's elite. On 29 December 1899, in the servants' quarters of Ralph's Hotel in the gritty northern suburb of Preston, Maggie Heffernan brought forth her firstborn child. She was unmarried, just twenty-two years old, and utterly alone. Unlike another birth in humble quarters long ago, this one passed without fanfare. No bright star marked its place; no wise men came calling. Yet this nativity also carried an omen, although not of salvation.

It was the prelude to a scandal.

Ralph's Junction Hotel Preston c.1900

CHAPTER 45

5 January 1900

The deep toll of the Parliament House clock echoed through the stone corridors as William Hill Irvine emerged from the Cabinet Room, leather case tucked beneath one arm. Outside, the summer sun poured through tall sash windows, casting sharp lines across the polished floor tiles.

Irvine, the newly appointed Attorney-General of the Colony of Victoria, paused for a moment. He adjusted his tie with the rote efficiency of a man whose mind was elsewhere, still ticking over the day's legal briefings and legislative reform proposals. A Queen's Counsel of formidable repute, Irvine had only just succeeded the legendary Isaac Isaacs, who had vacated the office of Attorney-General to take a national role on the eve of Federation.

He heard her before he saw her. The quick, deliberate footfalls on the tiles, the click of narrow heels echoing off the walls. When he turned, Mrs Kathleen Fraser was already upon him, extending her gloved hand with poise and confidence.

His brow furrowed as recognition stirred, but he hesitated to speak.

She dispensed with pleasantries and got straight to the matter at hand. She had a patriotic proposal. She wished to serve the British Empire in South Africa.

Irvine, momentarily at a loss, asked whether she had her nurse's certificate. She made her position clear—she wished to serve as a scout, spy, or sharpshooter. She was, she told him, an excellent shot, with unparalleled aim and unshakeable resolve.

She elaborated that the Boers, who fought from cover, had inflicted grave losses on British troops. A woman like herself, she argued—intelligent, determined, able to move unnoticed—could infiltrate enemy lines and return with information of military value.

Still searching for a diplomatic reply, Irvine ventured to ask how she proposed to reconcile such an expedition with her legal obligations here in Victoria. She replied that if she were killed in service, her bail bondsmen should be released from liability. If she survived, she would return to face court once her husband was fit to testify.

No doubt now looking for a polite way to disengage, Irvine advised that she take the matter to the Defence Department. Major-General Downes or Commander Collins would be better placed to assess her kind offer. And with that, she inclined her head, thanked him with perfect courtesy, and swept away down the corridor.

Irvine watched her go in silence.

Had he just spoken with a patriot, a fantasist, or a woman playing the boldest hand of her life?

CHAPTER 46

The Bendigo Advertiser described Mrs Fraser's approach to Mr Irvine as 'one of the most extraordinary communications which could at any time reach a Government department.'

But that was only the beginning.

Taking Irvine's advice at face value, she contacted the Defence Department. Commander Collins responded the next day with a polite but definitive rebuff: *Madam – Referring to your interview yesterday, and your offer to go on service in South Africa, I beg to inform you that the Minister for Defence, to whom I explained your proposal, is unable to say that any arrangement can be made by this department for sending you to the Cape. (Signed) ROBERT COLLINS, Secretary for Defence.*

Mrs Fraser was undeterred. 'It is a very nice letter,' she told the press, 'but, of course, as it does not grant what I desire, I am disappointed. I did want, and do still want, to go to South Africa for the purpose of assisting the British troops. I believe I am capable of assisting, as would be any person with brains and determination. But, anyhow, I'm not to be allowed to get away, that is evident.'

She hadn't finished.

Next, she sat down for interviews with any reporter willing to listen, and most were. The public, long fascinated by her, now hung on her every word.

To one reporter, she suggested that if necessary, she could disguise herself as a boy. She had always been a gymnast, she explained, and was therefore as strong as a man. She had no need to carry physical plans or documents, because she had a photographic memory. She would smuggle intelligence back across Boer lines hidden in a specially designed bombshell.

She still hadn't finished.

She cited examples from the American Civil War—Miss Beecher, who had performed valuable espionage for General Grant, and Miss Allan, who had done likewise for General Lee. If they could serve, why not her?

She kept going.

'If my disguise as a boy failed,' she said, 'I could instead pass as a Dutch vrouw.' She was, she explained, 'quite prepared to face the worst from a feminine standpoint—that of making myself look ugly enough to pass for a Boer belle.' It was the perfect trifecta, fusing humour, rampant jingoism, and unashamed vanity into a single, irresistible epigram.

The Age praised her 'strong right arm, stout heart, powers of endurance,' and 'skills at riding and shooting.' But, above all, it concluded, '*She possesses the feminine instinct for finding things out.*' *The Zeehan and Dundas Herald*, ever loyal since their *Lady Speculator* puff piece of 1896, now crowned her with a new epithet: *The St Kilda Sensation.*

And still she hadn't finished.

Careful to confirm that she was not boasting, Mrs Fraser told *The Herald* that in South Africa she could save the British from being led into such fearful ambushes as those at Nicholson's Neck, Stormberg, and Modder River. 'You think that a strange statement for a woman,' she continued, 'but I am not an ordinary woman by any means. I don't know what fear is. I am an exceptionally fine shot, a splendid horsewoman, I can swim well, and have tramped in the bush without food at a time when the men of my party had given in.'

And even then, she wasn't finished.

'While I was prospecting, I did not wear men's clothes. I had bloomers, and a short skirt coming down a little above the knees and fastening up the front with buttons. Of course, on the few occasions when I used a horse, I rode cross-saddle like a man.'

Victorian physicians had warned of the New Woman, whose voice grew *brusque*, whose manner was *assertive*, whose words *left nothing to the imagination*. Kathleen Fraser didn't reject this characterisation, she embodied it, wagering everything—her credibility, her reputation, her life—on the radical proposition that a woman could be strong, shrewd, scandalous, and still entirely feminine.

Then came the most elaborate pitch of all.

'Yes, I know you are going to say that it is nearly impossible for a woman to put on a man's clothes without detection. But, as I have said before, I am not an ordinary woman. When I was examined for life assurance, the doctor told me that I had one of the finest chests he had ever seen. I'm thirty-seven inches around under the arms, and I can expand. I've never worn corsets in my life.'

Undeterred, she doubled down: 'The grand secret of wearing men's clothes successfully is to make yourself thoroughly believe that you are a man. I have accustomed myself in my wanderings to that till the habit is second nature to me. At Evandale, I greatly desired to learn the bicycle, so I used to get up at three o'clock in the morning, dress myself in boy's clothes, and practice on the doctor's bicycle. Plenty of people saw me riding about, and no one ever suspected me of being anything else than I seemed.'

Melbourne's cross-dressing heroine still wasn't done.

For her grand finale, she returned to the pet subject of her prowess with firearms. Her final words carried a sick irony that seemed to escape her entirely: 'I am an exceptional shot with rifle, pistol, or revolver. When we were living at Evandale in Tasmania, I used to shoot wild ducks with a Martini-Henry rifle. My idea of shooting anything is to wait until it is almost out of sight. It seems more cruelty otherwise.'

For a society still unsure how to handle assertive women, Mrs Fraser gave them everything at once: danger, glamour, absurdity, and a backbone forged in steel. They could laugh, cheer, or scorn.

The one thing they couldn't do was look away.

CHAPTER 47

*You cannot hide murder under
the dust of outback roads, nor drown
it in the muddy creeks.*

— Henry Lawson, *A Camp Fire Yarn*, 1892

At 9.15 on the morning of Wednesday 17 January 1900, wharf labourer Peter Harris had already been at work three hours.

On the south bank of the Yarra, his gang toiled in heat and grime. The morning sun was already biting, with the mercury to climb to 39 degrees Celsius later that day. Harris wrinkled his nose as the stench of fish competed with the reek of animal hides bound for the North Melbourne tanneries. Streams of greasy runoff formed iridescent slicks on the river's surface, catching the sunlight in unnatural rainbows. Cargo cranes groaned under the strain of massive loads, their chains shrieking and clanking in harsh rhythm. The shouts of dock workers rang in Harris's ears, a cacophony that mirrored the river itself—turbid, relentless, and thoroughly unrefined.

From the corner of his eye, he saw something bobbing in the foul water. At first, it looked like any other floating waste: splintered wood, a tangle of reeds, an oil-darkened sack. As it drifted closer, something about its shape made him pause.

He squinted.

He wiped the sweat from his brow.

Realisation hit, and his stomach turned.

It was the body of a baby.

Melbourne Wharves, Yarra River 1905 (restored image).
AJ Campbell and Richard Daintree, Museums Victoria

CHAPTER 48

Maggie Heffernan's stomach twisted as she stepped back to let Detective Constable John Murray inside.

He was polite. Too polite.

She tried to keep her face still, to keep her hands from trembling as she answered his questions. The baby's paternal grandmother, Mrs Hardy, had come down from Sydney, she told him. She had taken the child back with her. She had accompanied them as far as Wangaratta. They had stayed at Allen's Hotel, and she had returned alone the next morning.

Murray nodded, scribbling in his notebook. Maggie could feel his eyes on her, weighing her words. Did he believe her? Should she ask for a solicitor? Was that something she could even do? He asked where Mrs Hardy lived.

'204 King Street, Sydney.' Maggie replied without hesitation. She kept her voice even. She had to sound sure.

'And have you heard from her since?'

She hesitated, just a breath too long. 'I'm expecting a letter.'

He seemed satisfied. For now.

He left, and Maggie pressed a hand to her chest, exhaling slowly. It was fine. It had to be fine.

Three days passed. Three days of dreading every knock at the door. When they came for her again, she knew. This time, Murray brought along a senior officer, Detective Sergeant Lawrence Gleeson. A seasoned veteran who would later be promoted to run the entire Victorian detective branch, Gleeson spoke with the weight of someone used to being obeyed. Maggie felt her breath shorten. They had made enquiries, Gleeson said. Her story about Allen's Hotel was untrue. There was no such address as 204 King Street in Sydney.

Her throat was dry. She forced herself to stay calm, willing her voice not to tremble as she said, 'I didn't stay at the hotel. I stayed at the station.'

Gleeson's gaze sharpened. 'What station?'

'The Wangaratta Railway Station.'

He didn't react, didn't move. Just watched her, letting the silence stretch too long. 'Did you stay at the Station Master's place?'

'No, we stayed in the paddock all night.'

Even as she said it, she knew how ridiculous it sounded. But they couldn't prove otherwise. Not yet.

Gleeson leaned forward, his voice heavy enough to pin her to the chair.

'It's no use telling us any more falsehoods. The child found in the Yarra is your child. Speak the truth and fear nothing.'

Maggie's breath caught. His words rang in her ears. But she could feel the fear rising, choking her. She swallowed hard.

'Yes, I know I did wrong.'

Gleeson didn't move. 'Speak the truth.'

Maggie's throat burned. Her eyes filled before she could stop them, and then the tears came.

CHAPTER 49

Selborne Chambers was Purves' domain.

The deep mahogany chair. The lingering scent of cigars. The studied ease with which he held court. Everything there revolved around him. Clerks scurried to his call, messengers hovered at the threshold, and junior barristers approached with the reverence of altar boys. Purves didn't just practise law there. He reigned.

Selborne was the nerve centre of Melbourne's legal precinct—a fortress of dark timber and bound volumes just a stone's throw from the Supreme Court. Exquisite gold aureoles gleamed from the faces of clocks mounted on columns at the entrance, prompting one journalist to quip that these embellishments symbolised 'the many guineas that have passed between litigants and counsel.'

It was here in Selborne Chambers that Kathleen Fraser met with her new legal team. Purves was their leader, ably assisted by solicitor Henry Hale Budd and junior barrister George James Dethridge.

Hale Budd was Purves' cousin, and the notorious perpetrator of a cruel family joke. In the lean early days of Purves' career, before a single brief had come his way, Hale Budd forged one and slipped it into his cousin's letterbox. Purves, unsuspecting, marched elated into the named solicitor's office, certain his career had finally begun. The solicitor glanced at the document and burst out laughing. The farce ended in a family fistfight.

Now in his late fifties, Hale Budd was well known in Melbourne's legal and sporting circles. He was a long-time committee member of the East Melbourne Cricket Club, on whose grounds the New Year's Eve Modder Bridge firework display had been staged.

Dethridge was the rising star of the Melbourne Bar. Barely yet thirty years of age, he was already gaining a fearsome reputation as a bulldog in cross-examination.

With Purves holding court and his crown prince Dethridge at his right hand, they tested Kathleen Fraser's evidence, probed the weaknesses in her case, and formulated a defence. They took instructions on every facet of the case: her marriage, her treatment at the hands of her husband, and her all-important state of mind at the time.

No transcripts survive from those confidential meetings. No shorthand notes. No trace in the record. Yet even as Purves and his team plotted their strategy, another verdict was already circulating — whispered in drawing rooms, printed in newspapers, shaping the trial before it began:

Hysteria.

Men could be drunk, violent, jealous, obsessive. They might gamble away a fortune, abandon their families, or strike their wives. But women? When they defied the script, when they shouted, sobbed, disobeyed, or fought back, the verdict was already written. They were hysterical. Irrational. Mad.

The public was primed to believe it. The jury might forgive it. And the Kew Lunatic Asylum, a vast and imposing facility opened in 1872, always had room for one more.

In medical texts, the symptoms of hysteria included fainting, convulsions, hallucinations, muscular twitching, cries in the night, obsessive speech, even blasphemy. Anything that deviated from the norms of wifehood, motherhood, silence and softness was ripe for medical framing.

The causes were equally revealing. Darwin had written that women were biologically less evolved than men—emotionally sensitive, morally weaker, prone to irrationality. Henry Maudsley, the leading British psychiatrist, warned that 'the mind of woman is always threatened with danger from the reverberations of her reproductive system.' And newcomer Sigmund Freud was now framing hysteria as the result of repressed female sexuality.

Throughout the British Empire, husbands could and did commit their wives to lunatic asylums with little more than a doctor's note. One woman was institutionalised for reading novels, another for refusing to have sex. A minister's wife was confined by her husband because she disagreed with his theology.

Within this landscape, everything about Mrs Fraser signalled the same conclusion. She was loud and unconventional. She had thrown bricks and a chisel, dropped wood on a workman's head, slapped her husband with a paintbrush ... and of course, shot him in the head.

In the end, her trial would become more than a contest of evidence. It would be a test of society's willingness to believe in a woman's agency — to see her acting not as a vessel of hysteria, but with intent.

Was she insane, or just angry?

Was she delusional, or just defiant?

And could the legal system, steeped in male authority and feminine myth, bring itself to see the difference?

CHAPTER 50

Mrs Fraser's committal hearing was convened on the morning of Friday 2 February 1900 at the St Kilda Police Court.

Edwin Corr, the erstwhile Will drafter and bicycle injury lawyer, was back in Court for his client Dr Fraser. That awkward introduction at the bicycle races had certainly paid off.

Like any complainant in a criminal trial, Dr Fraser was not technically a party to the proceedings. The case was between the Crown and Mrs Fraser, so Corr had no standing to appear. But he had a plan – a bold guerilla tactic that would require timing, nerve, and more front than the Federal Coffee Palace.

The purpose of the Committal hearing was for the magistrates to hear the prosecution's case and decide if there was enough evidence to commit the accused to trial in the Supreme Court. Accordingly, the defence case wouldn't be heard that day. The magistrates would also re-consider the question of bail, which was when Corr planned to make his move.

The Courthouse was heaving, full to the brim with eager onlookers. The young Mayor Kemp was presiding once again. He was flanked by a worthy panel of magistrates: Hennessy, Panter, Marks, and finally Moore, who had overseen Dr Fraser's original Dying Man's Deposition. None of them were lawyers by training; they were lay magistrates and local dignitaries.

George James Dethridge lounged at the bar table as if he were enjoying a smoke night at the Melbourne Club. Hale Budd sat behind him, the two taking the traditional separate roles of barrister and solicitor.

Purves wasn't there. The King of the Melbourne Bar wouldn't stoop so low as to appear in the Magistrates Court. He would appear only in the Supreme Court, at trial.

Fashionable in a black dress, Mrs Fraser sat in the dock at Dethridge's request—a move straight from his master's repertoire. Her eyes shone with intensity as she looked around, unfazed by the attention. Mrs Howard, her sister from Sydney, gave a supportive smile from the public gallery.

The crowd parted as two medical orderlies wheeled Dr Fraser into the courtroom, his legs useless since the shooting. His left arm, swathed in a sling, rested uncomfortably on his lap whilst his slippered feet, wrapped in thick bandages, hung limp from the wheelchair. His brother-in-law Mr Pennington, having recently arrived from England, followed behind. Both kept their gaze fixed on the bench, refusing to look at Mrs Fraser in the dock.

Once again, Inspector Crampton appeared as Police Prosecutor.

Crampton moved through the evidence without fuss. In cross-examination, Dethridge played with Crampton's witnesses like a cat might play with a mouse, landing a few blows just for the sport of it. This wasn't the trial. For Dethridge, it was just an opportunity to understand the prosecution's case, preen and strut in front of the solicitors, and soften up the witnesses ahead of the main event.

The magistrates duly committed Mrs Fraser to trial in the Supreme Court of Victoria for the crime of attempted murder.

Dethridge applied for bail, believing this to be a formality. Mrs Fraser had already been bailed numerous times before, always on the same terms: a recognisance of £1000 from her personally, and £500 from each of Mr O'Malley and Mr Ferne.

Without hesitation, Crampton confirmed that the Police had no objections.

Corr's heart thumped in his chest as Crampton took his seat. It was his moment.

As if catapulted by a spring, he leapt to his feet.

Every head in the room turned.

The game was about to change.

CHAPTER 51

'Your Worships, I represent Dr Fraser' said Corr, blood pounding in his temples. 'I must oppose bail. Dr Fraser is in fear for his life!' His voice rang out with unexpected authority, echoing through the packed courtroom. 'He is living under an assumed name because of this fear.'

For a split second, silence gripped the room. Every eye locked onto Corr.

Then came the sound.

The scrape of the dock chair cut through the courtroom like a knife across porcelain. All heads snapped toward the dock. The chair had been flung back, and Mrs Fraser was on her feet, eyes ablaze.

'Then, if so—' she roared, her voice cracking with fury as she clung to the dock rails.

The crowd leaned in.

'SIT DOWN AND BE QUIET!'

Hale Budd had shot to his feet, turning on her with the ferocity of a drill sergeant dressing down a mutinous private soldier.

A taut second passed. The whole courtroom seemed to hold its breath.

Then, slowly, still gripping the dock rails, Mrs Fraser lowered herself back into the chair.

Without missing a beat, Corr pressed on. 'Might Dr Fraser once again answer a few questions, your Worships? From the comfort of his chair, if it pleases the Court?'

The magistrates exchanged glances before nodding in silent agreement.

Corr's throat felt tight as he swallowed hard. Now that he had their attention, he needed to capitalise on it. 'Dr Fraser,' Corr began, his voice steady but firm, 'do you recall when the defendant visited you in hospital on the 4th of November?'

'Yes,' the doctor confirmed, 'Very much so.'

'What happened during that visit?'

Dr Fraser hesitated for a moment, rubbing a hand over his pallid face. 'Oh, she started the usual thing,' he said, his words clipped. 'Wanted me to go live with her again. Said I should give her money. I refused, of course.' His tone was cold, indifferent.

'And how did she respond?' Corr asked, although of course he already knew the answer.

'She said she wished to God she had finished me off altogether, and was sorry she hadn't.'

The courtroom shuddered with the weight of his words. A murmur swept through the gallery.

Corr continued. 'And what about her language, Dr Fraser? How did she speak to you?'

Dr Fraser's lips twisted into something that might have been a smile. 'Pretty free, as usual. She called me all the opprobrious epithets she could lay her tongue to.'

With painstaking attention to detail, Corr then took his client through his wife's other two unhinged visits to his hospital bedside.

'Are you genuinely afraid of her?'

'Yes. Once I even complained about her to a Constable.'

At this, Dethridge practically leapt across the bar table. 'What is his name? You say you complained to a Constable. Who was it?'

'I ... I don't know all the Constables in St Kilda, Sir...'

'Come now...' Dethridge sneered, holding out his arms in shrugging motion to the bench.

'Come now be damned, you're nothing but a bully,' the doctor spat back.

It was a strange interaction. The court would soon hear that it was Senior Constable George Doran Williams, Dr Fraser's longstanding friend, to whom he had complained. Williams himself was in the room, waiting to give evidence.

Corr jumped in to protect his client. 'He is not at all well,' he told the magistrates. 'Allowance should be made for his condition.'

Dethridge was having none of it. 'I claim the right to examine the witness as I think fit,' he thundered, 'so that the truth may be gained.'

The young barrister had summoned the higher creed long professed by men like Purves: that a barrister's duty was not to spare feelings, but to test, to probe, and to strip the truth bare whatever the cost. Unused to such confident assertion of an advocate's rights, the bench yielded without debate — a reminder of the unspoken authority wielded by gentlemen of the bar over lay magistrates.

Dethridge's dander was now up. He couldn't resist launching another salvo, blasting Dr Fraser from all angles. None of his shots hit the target.

Corr seized the moment. 'Don't just take the informant's word for it, Your Worships. I have three witnesses waiting here in the Court to corroborate what he says.' He waved towards the back of the Court, where Senior Constable Williams stood with John Robins and Mrs Evans.

Dethridge flashed an angry look and retreated to his chair.

The witnesses were sworn in, and one by one they confirmed what Dr Fraser had said.

Dethridge wasn't used to being outshone, and especially not by an Amalgam. It was time to seize back control of his bail application.

'Your Worships,' he said, in a patronising tone, 'it would be ridiculous to deprive the accused of her liberty because of *vague fears* such as had been expressed. She is an excitable woman, and her language is perhaps sometimes overstrung. But that language is a matter of taste, and doubtless her husband has become accustomed to it.'

Corr then gave the speech of his career.

'Your Worships, the accused has told a policeman that she believes in fate, and that she is driven by its irresistible urges. A woman like that must simply not be released on bail. Fate might, if she were to be freed, drive her to inflict upon the doctor a fate that he would not wish to meet. How can you, we, or anyone be sure that she will not be seized by such an impulse at any moment between now and the trial?'

The bench retired for no more than five minutes. When they returned, faces expressionless, Mayor Kemp finally spoke. 'In this case we will not take the responsibility of granting bail. Bail is therefore refused.'

Mrs Fraser collapsed forward, face buried in her hands, her sobs raw and unrelenting.

'With respect to Your Worships,' said Dethridge in a tone which was anything but respectful, 'we must now take this matter immediately to the Supreme Court.'

One of the most effective ways for a barrister to cow a local bench was to postulate that their rulings would be reviewed, and likely overturned, by a higher authority. Dethridge knew it, and delivered the threat with quiet disdain. But it was to no avail. The magistrates held firm.

Seizing the moment, Corr made one final request. 'Your Worships, may I also ask that custody of the child be given to Dr Fraser, given his wife is to be remanded in custody? His sister is with him, and the child will be well cared for.'

But the bench of the St. Kilda Police Court had been pushed far enough. Mr Moore gave a raw, defensive outburst.

'You have forced the accused to go to the Supreme Court for bail, now you can go to the Supreme Court for the child.'

The record is silent on how Dr Fraser or Pennington responded to Moore's pronouncement, but as events soon proved, the matter was far from over.

CHAPTER 52

Once she had stopped crying, Maggie Heffernan made the following statement:

On Monday the 15th January I left Mrs Cameron's Home, Armadale, about 10.30am with my baby boy. I went to Melbourne by train.

On arrival in Melbourne about 12.30 pm same day I went to Preston by train. I got out of the train at Northcote. I intended to go to Ralph's Hotel Preston for my box but I changed my mind and returned by train to Melbourne with my baby.

On my arrival in Melbourne I walked about the town with the child. About 5 pm I went into the Treasury Gardens where I gave the baby a drink from the breast. I then went to the Women's Christian Association at the corner of Spring and Little Flinders Streets where I tried to get a bed for the night for myself and baby. I had only two shillings in money on me then. I could not get a bed there. A lady there told me to go to a similar institution in Flinders Street where they took in women with babies. I went to that institution and was there told that they did not take in women with babies. I tried 2 hotels and the Victoria Coffee Palace in Collins Street. I could not get a bed at either of the hotels but I could get a bed at the Coffee Palace for 2/6. As I had only 2/8 I went away but not before they had told me that they could not give me a bed for two shillings.

I then spoke to a woman in Collins Street who told me that I could get a bed at a Restaurant in Bourke Street near the Parliament House where I got a bed for myself and baby.

I left there about 9 o'clock next morning. I was given a cup of tea before I left there.

I walked down the street and bought an Argus which I read to see if I could [find] a situation anywhere. I then went over Prince's Bridge and into the Botanical Gardens. I remained in the Gardens with the baby till about 11 o'clock.

I then returned along St Kilda Road to some steps near Princes Bridge. The steps led down to the south side of the Yarra River. I walked up and down the riverside for about an hour. I then sat down with the baby. The baby was clothed with a little gown and a small piece of flannel only. The flannel was of a white colour and the gown was white too. I sat close up to the edge of the water. I took the gown from off the baby. I took off the flannel too. I then let the baby drop gently into the river. The baby was alive when I dropped it into the river. I did not look to see whether the baby sank or not.

I then walked away carrying in my hand the gown and flannel. It would be about one o'clock in the day then. I then went to Flinders Street Station got a ticket and travelled by rail to Preston where I went to Ralph's Hotel. I stayed there that night 16th of January.

The foregoing statement covering eight pages in this book and each of which page is signed by me is my statement and it is true in every particular.

That statement was made of my own free will and accord and without hope of favour or fear of threats.

Maggie Heffernan

They took her in a hansom cab to the Police Station. The ride was silent except for the clatter of hooves on the road. Maggie stared out of the window, hands clenched in her lap.

At the station, they read her statement back to her. Gleeson's voice was flat, emotionless. 'You are charged with murder.'

The words fell between them like a stone into deep water, and Maggie felt herself sinking along with them.

As they led her away, she offered no resistance. The cell door clanged shut, the sound ringing in her ears. She was truly alone now, with no river to carry her woes away.

CHAPTER 53

Tuesday 5 February 1900

The thunderous banging on the front door sent a jolt through the house.

Mrs Howard froze. Her little niece Katie, curled in her lap, looked up with wide, uncertain eyes.

Mrs Howard's arm tightened protectively around her. She forced a reassuring smile and smoothed the girl's hair, her gaze flickering toward the darkened hallway.

She had been expecting this.

Another knock — louder now, more forceful.

Mrs Howard put down the storybook, scooped Katie into her arms, and hurried upstairs. She pressed a quick kiss to the girl's forehead and set her gently on the bed.

'Stay here. Don't move.'

She turned and went downstairs to take up her post in the back parlour, just as they had planned.

Whatever was about to happen, she was ready.

CHAPTER 54

Mrs Howard had feared it might come to this.

Ever since the magistrates sent her sister back to gaol and refused Dr Fraser's custody application, she had been on high alert.

She was staying with little Katie at Mrs McCormick's home on Mary Street, St Kilda, just a few doors down from the now-finished Resarf Terrace.

Her heart ached at the thought of her sister languishing in that bluestone hell hole, but the law had its process, its proper channels. Tomorrow at the Supreme Court, Mr Dethridge would ask Justice Hood to release Kathleen. She had to stay strong until then.

They had prepared for this moment. Mrs McCormick had been particularly vigilant, keeping an eye on strangers who had been seen lurking around the street. They had bolted the gates and checked the locks. 'This place is starting to feel like Ladysmith,' she'd quipped, referring to the besieged town in South Africa that was dominating the headlines.

Still, Mrs Howard hadn't expected it to happen quite so brazenly.

Another sharp rap on the front door made her stiffen. One of the servant girls froze, eyes darting to Mrs Howard for direction. In a whispered voice, she told her to see who it was.

The girl crept toward the door. Before she could reach it, another knock rang out, louder, more insistent. The girl opened the door just an inch, putting her full weight behind it.

Through the crack in the door, she saw a tall, well-dressed man. He stood with an air of authority, as if the street belonged to him. 'I need to see Mrs Howard' he drawled, each syllable loaded with smug English condescension.

The girl swallowed hard, gripping the edge of the door. 'She's not here.'

The man smiled, sharp and mocking. 'Come now, you know where she is. I must see her.'

The girl slammed the door in his face.

There was a metallic clank as he pushed open the letterbox from outside the door and peered through.

'Who are you?' called the frightened girl.

'I'm Mr You-Know-Who, from You-Know-Where,' he replied, with a dripping sarcasm that made Mrs Howard's skin prickle.

A moment later, his voice came again. He was shouting now, his voice echoing down the corridor to where Mrs Howard still sat, frozen. 'I know she's in there. I've come for the child.'

Then the noise started again, as he alternately rattled the door back and forth, knocked hard, and shouted his demands for them to hand over the child.

The plucky servant girl bolted to the backyard. They'd planned for this. Rather than risk opening the locked gate, she scrambled up the eight-foot galvanised fence and dropped to the road behind. Then she ran straight to the home of Mr Joseph Toohey, former superintendent of Police.

Upstairs, a second servant girl was also deploying as per her mistress's instructions. She lifted Katie from her bed and locked her inside the master bedroom. Then, she stepped out onto the front balcony, looking down at the man below. He stood on the footpath, arms crossed, studying her with an unsettling, detached gaze.

'I want to get the child!' he called up.

'You won't get her!' she shot back, hands shaking but voice strong.

He scowled. 'I demand her!'

'Then you can go on demanding,' came the insolent retort.

Neighbours were beginning to gather outside, peering from windows and craning their necks to see what the fuss was about. Mr Toohey had arrived, taking in the situation with sharp eyes, accompanied by his son and a neighbour.

Emboldened, Mrs Howard finally moved from her seat in the back room and walked through to the front parlour. She paused just short of the window, drawing a slow breath and holding it. Then she stepped forward and looked out.

Through the glass, she saw Mr Toohey step up and confront the man.

'Who are you?' Toohey asked.

'Pennington's my name. Brother-in-law of Dr Fraser.' He paused, letting the name linger. 'I have come for the child.'

Low murmurs stirred amongst the onlookers. Everyone knew the Fraser case, and now it was playing out right here, in front of them. Mrs Howard's blood must have boiled. Dr Fraser, who hadn't even spoken with her since the incident, who had dismissed her from the Alfred saying she talks too much, had sent his brother-in-law to do what the court had refused.

Toohey's son and another man stepped in, blocking Pennington's path. He hesitated, eyes darting between the men and the darkened windows above. For a moment, it seemed like he might try to force his way in. But he turned and retreated to his cab.

Mrs Howard exhaled. She went upstairs and unlocked the bedroom door. Katie ran straight into her arms.

But it wasn't over.

Less than half an hour later, he returned.

Mrs Howard had moved to the window, keeping watch, when she spotted a lone figure lingering on the footpath, his posture eerily familiar. She narrowed her eyes. Pennington had changed his coat and swapped his hat. Did he really believe that this meagre disguise would make him unrecognisable? Or was this just another form of intimidation? Either way, Pennington simply stood there, watching.

He stayed like that for minutes, shifting slightly, trying to blend in with the onlookers still murmuring about the night's events. And then, as if sensing her gaze, he turned and walked away.

Tomorrow, they would face Dr Fraser and his family again in Court.

But tonight?

Tonight, they had won.

CHAPTER 55

Wednesday 6 February 1900

A judge is a law student who marks his own examination papers.

— H.L. Mencken, American journalist, 1920s

Corr rushed down the hallway toward Justice Hood's chambers, breath coming in sharp, uneven bursts. Late—for this of all days. He could have cursed himself.

This wasn't just another Police Court bail hearing. Today Corr would appear before a Supreme Court judge. For a jack-of-all-trades Amalgam, this was a shot at the big league. And he was arriving in a fluster.

At least he had a strong case. Three witnesses had given evidence of Mrs Fraser's unhinged behaviour, and one of them was George Doran Williams, a policeman, the gold standard of testimonial credibility.

Better still, Corr had a legal precedent. Not from some dusty old English tome, either. He had found a recent Australian case, decided by Justice Thomas A'Beckett, Hood's respected brother judge of the Victorian Supreme Court. A man whose blood was so blue that his family claimed descendancy from the original A'Beckett himself, Saint Thomas of Canterbury, the famed Archbishop martyred in 1170.

Less than a month ago, Justice A'Beckett had refused bail to one Dr Lalor, accused of attempted murder, because of concerns that he may commit further violent acts. The case had attracted wide press coverage. Hood would surely have been aware of it. Indeed, he had likely discussed it with A'Beckett himself over drinks in Chambers.

The defendant was the only son of the late Peter Lalor, the politician and lauded leader of the Eureka Rebellion. The case had been a scandal. The intoxicated physician had attempted to shoot Ballarat auctioneer John Coghlan in broad daylight, right in the middle of conducting a public auction. Dr Lalor later claimed that he couldn't remember the incident. Coghlan had given evidence that he was scared for his life and for that of his wife. Sending Dr Lalor back down to the cells, Justice A'Beckett had pronounced, 'If a man went about drinking, committing assaults, and forgetting about it, then it was as well that he should be locked up where he could not get a drink and not be a danger to anyone.'

As he burst into Hood's chambers, Corr was met with a roomful of familiar faces. Dethridge sat confidently, calm and collected. Mr Guiness from the Crown Solicitor's office was also present, as was Mr Pennington. It is not known whether Mrs Howard was there.

Everyone turned to stare as Corr walked in. Pennington rushed over to him. 'Where were you?' he whispered, in a refined drawl that seemed too loud in the quiet chambers. 'The judge has adjourned for ten minutes to wait for you,' he added.

Precisely three minutes later, Hood strode into the room. The temperature dropped. He moved fast, a blur of robes and impatience, wasting no time on pleasantries.

'Good morning, gentlemen,' Hood began. Hood fixed his steely gaze on Corr. 'We are here today for a bail application. I've read the affidavits. Proceed.'

MR JUSTICE HOOD

Hood was known in legal circles as *The Lightning Judge*. Some folks said his nickname praised his ability to grasp the salient points of a case and plough through a significant caseload at speed. Others said that he progressed matters too quickly, at the expense of justice.

Mr Guiness led off, declaring that the Crown had no objection to Mrs Fraser's application for bail. After all, she had been granted bail numerous times before without issue. Hood nodded vigorously in agreement, responding that this was a very sensible position. 'And indeed,' he pronounced, skewering Corr with a withering look, 'the only position that you can take up.'

Not even the Lightning Judge would make up his mind before the hearing had even started, surely? Corr stood up and prepared to dazzle, just as he had before the magistrates last week.

'Your honour,' Corr projected with confidence as he approached the bench, 'on behalf of the complainant, Dr Fraser, I object to bail being granted.'

The Lightning Judge slapped him straight down. 'I don't know what Dr Fraser has to do with it,' he barked, referring to the fact that Dr Fraser, the complainant, was not himself a party to the proceedings. 'I'm not even sure that you have the right to appear, Mr Corr.'

Corr had come prepared to argue the substantive issues, but now Hood had ambushed him with a procedural matter. Was he being treated this way because he was an Amalgam?

Most of the current Supreme Court bench had been barristers at the time of amalgamation. They had joined the Bar Association's attempt to freeze out the Amalgams from higher practice. A decade on, the spirit of that exclusion still lingered.

Corr persisted. 'Your Honour, there is a case...'

'About whether you have a right of audience in these proceedings?'

'No your Honour, a recent case on bail. The matter of Dr Lalor in the Ballarat Court.'

Corr didn't have a copy of the judgement to hand up to Justice Hood. On the backfoot already, he impressed on the judge that the case was well known. It had been heard only last month before Justice A'Beckett. 'In that case,' Corr explained, 'his Honour had permitted the victim to make application to oppose bail, as he feared for his life.'

Hood cut him off with a single, dismissive line. 'I don't see what that has to do with it.'

Corr battled on stubbornly. 'We say that there are circumstances which, if brought under your Honour's notice, might induce your Honour not to grant bail. If the prisoner were out, some offence against justice might be committed.'

The Judge then drew a curious parallel. 'Do you mean to say that in a case of larceny, bail should be refused because the accused might commit another larceny?'

It was a well-worn doctrinal stance: that the sole purpose of bail was to ensure the accused returned to face trial—not to prevent further offences. But in this case, the stakes were higher than for larceny. A man was in fear for his life.

Dethridge tendered affidavit evidence on behalf of Mrs Fraser. Flatly contradicting the sworn testimony of three other witnesses, in her affidavit she denied ever threatening her husband at Mrs Evans' hospital. 'The real reason for her husband opposing bail is transparent,' Dethridge argued. 'He wants custody of their child.'

'There is, of course, another option available to your client,' said Hood to Corr, a thin smile appearing on his lips. 'If Dr Fraser is concerned about his safety, he could relocate back to Tasmania until his wife's trial.'

The injured man couldn't even walk into court unaided, let alone make the journey to Tasmania and back. Reading the room, Corr realised that pointing this out to the Lightning Judge might just make things worse.

'An accused person is presumed to be innocent until the verdict at the trial,' Hood pronounced. 'The *only ground* to lock up an accused person is to make sure that he will appear at the trial.'

He stared hard at Corr, daring the Amalgam to challenge him.

Corr knew that the legal principle so confidently articulated by Hood had originated in his own head. Under the law, Hood in fact had a broad discretion to grant or deny bail. But what was the point of correcting him?

Hood continued, his voice thick with condescension, telling Corr that *his client* had mistaken the very grounds on which he was entitled to oppose the application. He might as well have put a dunce's hat on Corr's head, stood him in the corner, and encouraged Dethridge to flick rubber bands at him.

'If Dr Fraser had come forward as a member of the public,' the Judge continued, 'stating that it was probable that the accused might abscond, then I could have considered his case.'

As if pointing out to a child where the crayons are kept, Hood also explained that Dr Fraser had another remedy available. He could apply to have Mrs Fraser bound over to keep the peace. Struggling now to remain deferential, Corr snapped back that this would be little comfort after the husband had been shot. Again.

Corr's point was well made. Only last year, a violent offender named Richard Hammel—recently bailed out of Melbourne Gaol—had waited outside his estranged wife's home as she returned from the theatre. When she saw him, the terrified woman fled to a nearby hansom cab. He smashed its windows and dragged her out by the hair. He stood over her, threatening to kill her in front of their daughter. Hammel was bound over to keep the peace, on a recognisance of ten pounds.

Three days later he came back. He broke in through her window and bludgeoned her with an iron bar. That time, bail was denied.

Perhaps the memory of the Hammel case stirred something in Corr. Or perhaps he had reached the limit of what he could stomach from Hood.

Either way, something snapped.

Corr straightened, his voice louder now, his deference thinning. Against every instinct of self-preservation, he dared to strike back.

'Will your Honour read the evidence?' he shot across the bench. Not a question. A challenge. The room fell still. Before Hood could respond, Corr reminded him that only minutes after Mrs Fraser had shot her husband, she had claimed that she had an irresistible impulse which prompted her to do certain things.

'Then take her to a lunatic asylum,' came the cold response.

By now, Corr knew he was fighting a lost cause. He was a trespasser in their house, and no amount of law or reason would change that. Still, Pennington's eyes were on him—steady, expectant, heavy with hope. That silent demand no advocate can ignore: *do something*.

Corr squared his shoulders and gave it one final push.

He repeated his original speech to the magistrates almost word for word. 'I think,' Corr concluded, once more with sufficient control to dress his anger in courtroom courtesies, 'it is a case where your Honour could exercise your discretion, and say that no bail should be allowed.'

Hood's face was resolute. 'Bail has been granted before, and

I see no reason to refuse it now, the Crown being willing to accept the same.' There was no pause, no hesitation. 'The only object in locking an accused person up is to make sure that he will appear for trial. She has had bail four or five times, and I don't see any reason for withdrawing it now.'

'Application granted.'

CHAPTER 56

In the weeks leading up to her trial, Mrs Fraser and Mr Hale Budd visited Purves and Dethridge at Selborne Chambers to discuss a key strategic question: would she give evidence at trial?

Under the laws of the day, she had three options.

She could remain silent. The law didn't compel her to testify, and the burden of proof rested with the Crown. But silence could be risky. Jurors often took it as an admission of guilt, despite a judge's clear instructions to the contrary.

She could take the stand. That would let her speak directly to the jury, to tell them what her husband had done to her, the fear she lived in, and her state of mind on the day. But there was a price. Once sworn in, Finlayson would cross-examine her. He would press her on inconsistencies, expose contradictions, and attack her credibility. If she faltered even once, the damage could be fatal.

Her third option was the dock statement. This would allow her to address the jury from the dock—unsworn, and free from cross-examination. The dock statement had been introduced in England and adopted in the colonies during the late nineteenth century. The idea was to give a voice to those too vulnerable, uneducated or shaken to face questions from the Crown Prosecutor. But there was a trade-off. Judges were required to instruct the jury that the dock statement carried less weight than sworn testimony from the witness box.

Dock statements could also backfire spectacularly. They could look contrived. Manipulative. Weak. Critics sometimes called them 'a coward's refuge.' Such perceptions could sway jurors, casting doubt on the defendant's credibility and courage.

There's an old adage in the legal profession: the lawyer shows the cards, but the client plays the hand.

Ultimately, the decision rested with Mrs. Fraser.

Yet like a carnival grifter dealing a stacked deck, Purves knew there was only one option his client was ever going to take.

CHAPTER 57

By 1900, the newly-elevated Charles Braine Finlayson QC had become the quiet backbone of the Crown Law Office in his measured and incorruptible way. Some traced his rigour to his Scottish education; others to his childhood in Jamaica where he had witnessed first-hand the injustices meted out to plantation workers by the ruling elite.

If Jamaica had taught him what unchecked power looked like, Freemasonry offered the antidote: a brotherhood built on restraint, ritual, and reverence for truth. Within Finlayson's own Royal Arch order, the symbol of the Knight Templar embodied that creed: a guardian of virtue who drew his sword only in defence, never in anger.

For Finlayson, this philosophy extended into the courtroom. He prosecuted fairly and with honour. In the register of correspondence at the Crown Law Office, his directions appeared month after month, recommending prosecutions be dropped for lack of evidence.

It was a noble ideal. Since the 1820s, courts had commended prosecutors who exercised their powers tenderly. In one celebrated early Victorian trial, the Attorney-General voluntarily introduced defence evidence and highlighted flaws in the prosecution's own case—a gesture so noble it drew praise from opposing counsel.

But in colonial Australia, this ideal was rarely the reality.

Prosecutions have long mirrored contemporary fears and prejudices. And in the fledgling colonies of the Antipodes, prosecutors often saw themselves as the last line of defence against disorder, social decay, and the decline of British standards. In trials that touched a nerve such as cases involving bushrangers, political radicals, or defiant women, zeal often displaced restraint.

The 1880 prosecution of Ned Kelly had been one such case. Kelly had killed a policeman and was, in the eyes of many, an enemy of civilisation. His prosecutor even questioned whether Kelly's lawyer should be permitted to argue his case at all. In another bushranger trial, the prosecutor declared that the law must make an example of the accused men, lamenting that their behaviour was 'beyond the pale of the law' and expressing his sincere hope that they would hang.

It was in the shadow of this legacy that, early in the year 1900, Finlayson would face his sternest test yet as Crown Prosecutor. He had three capital trials to run, each demanding that he remain steady while the world around him lost its head.

The first was John Foster. A jealous lover, caught mid-attack in a daylight stabbing.

The second was Maggie Heffernan. A servant girl, accused of drowning her newborn child.

The third was Kathleen Fraser, the St Kilda Sensation. A case so swamped in media frenzy and gendered intrigue that the facts struggled to be heard above the noise.

Three lives on the line.

Three emotionally-charged trials about state of mind, motive, and moral judgment.

And three chances for Melbourne's newest QC to uphold the quiet, exacting creed of his office.

CHAPTER 58

In February 1900, the war in South Africa continued to dominate the headlines. Grim news arrived that Melbourne's own hero, the dashing acting Captain Tim McInerney, had been wounded and captured in a skirmish near Rensburg. He was now languishing in a Boer Prisoner of War camp.

Photo. by T. Humphrey.]
CAPTAIN T. M. McINERNEY,
Of the First Victorian Contingent, who was wounded at Rensburg and captured by the Boers. He is a brother of Dr. McInerney, Warden of the Melbourne University.

From *Table Talk*, Thursday 22 February 1900

But Finlayson had no time for news from the Cape. He had three capital trials to run.

His new embroidered silk robes swished with quiet grandeur as he rose from his seat to prosecute the first matter on the list: *Regina v. John Foster*.

From the front row of the public gallery, Amy Alice Peterson watched with visible enjoyment. She sat as close to the dock as decorum allowed, flashing triumphant glances in the defendant's direction. Her conduct proved so disruptive that court officials had to intervene. 'She was repressed by the Police' reported the *Boulder Evening Star*, 'but her satisfaction was none the less apparent.'

Justice Hodges presided. Foster was represented by Mr Field-Barrett, a court-appointed Amalgam better known for his missteps than his advocacy.

Two years earlier, Field-Barrett had himself faced criminal charges for receiving stolen money. Charges that were eventually dismissed, thanks to the silver tongue of his barrister, James Liddell Purves QC. Days after the Foster trial, Field-Barrett would again be named and shamed in the newspapers for failing to appear in court to represent another client.

MR. JUSTICE HODGES.

Finlayson did his usual thorough job. He laid out the facts: how Foster had bought the butcher's knife on the day of the incident, how he had terrified his victim by breaking into her home and smashing through a glass door, how Peterson and her child had fled into the street. He described how Foster pursued her with a singular focus, knife in hand, striking several blows before he was arrested. And how he had carried the extraordinary armoury of a butcher's knife, two cutthroat razors, and a revolver.

The parallels with Mrs Fraser's case were striking. Both defendants had carried weapons. Both had made clear threats beforehand. Both had attacked in broad daylight, in public places. Both were obsessed with reconciling with their spouse. Although as far as reconciliation was concerned, Foster seemed more honest and less strategic. He had always been obsessed with Amy Alice Peterson. By contrast, Mrs Fraser's apparent desire to reunite with her husband emerged only after she was arrested for shooting him.

Foster did not plead insanity. Finlayson may have felt a flicker of relief. An insanity plea might have afforded at least some prospect of an acquittal. The mad frenzy with which he attacked his victim—unprovoked, and in broad daylight— could have suggested a disease of the mind.

But even so, Foster would have faced two problems with an insanity defence: he was male, and he was working class. Hysteria—the so-called 'daughter disease of capitalism'— belonged to educated society ladies, not to men who dug sewerage trenches for the Melbourne and Metropolitan Board of Works.

Foster instead pleaded not guilty on the ground that he

didn't intend to harm Peterson. A defence which was laughably weak on its face. If that was the case, asked Finlayson, then why did he take an arsenal of weapons to Howard Street? He was simply in the habit of carrying them, Foster replied. And why, the prosecutor asked, was he holding the butcher's knife when he grabbed Peterson? He had originally been carrying it in his pocket he said, but it jumped out when he started running. So, he held it in his hand 'to save losing it.'

Finlayson didn't ask any more questions. He didn't need to.

The fatal blow came from Foster's landlady, Isabella Young. In a chilling echo of the threats made by Mrs Fraser, Foster had told her that if he couldn't get Peterson's child, he'd 'do for' the mother, then shoot himself. Mrs Young later tried to recant her testimony, claiming she'd been the worse for drink. But by then, the damage had already been done.

The jury retired at 3:37 p.m.

Conventional wisdom said that quick juries convict, and slow juries acquit. If they were back before dinner, Foster was done for.

The clock ticked.

By 4:40 p.m. the door opened. Just over an hour had passed. They had their verdict. The foreman stood. 'Guilty.'

Quick juries convict, slow juries acquit.

Justice Hodges didn't mince his words. Staring down from the bench, he pronounced that Foster had committed a wicked, cowardly and premeditated assault with a murderous weapon on a defenceless woman. As he donned the black cap, he recited the time-honoured words:

'You will be taken from this place to a lawful prison, and thence to a place of execution, to be hanged there by the neck until you are dead. And may the Lord have mercy on your soul.'

Foster turned to Peterson, a twisted smirk curling at the edges of his lips.

He gave her a slow, mocking bow, then raised his hand in a jaunty wave as if bidding farewell at a Sunday picnic.

He turned and descended to the cells.

CHAPTER 59

As the ink dried on John Foster's death warrant, another defendant stood in the dock at the Supreme Court: a servant girl accused of drowning her newborn in the Yarra.

Moral crusaders across Melbourne were at the same time railing against Dr O'Hara's Silenette, condemning contraception as a threat to public decency. But the Heffernan case revealed the other side of the story: the brutal cost borne by women with no access to safe choices.

There was little press interest in her trial. The shooting of a well-to-do doctor by his theatrical wife commanded headlines; the quiet drowning of a bastard child by a housemaid did not.

Justice Hodges presided once again. Charles Braine Finlayson QC returned for the Prosecution. Heffernan was represented by court-appointed barrister Sir Bryan O'Loghlen QC, a former Premier and Attorney-General of Victoria. On paper, O'Loghlen had all the right credentials. But he was now seventy-two years old, and long past his prime.

According to the *Australian Women's Sphere*, a mistake had been made. Heffernan was meant to have retained another barrister, a man at the top of his game, with a wealthy donor lined up to cover the fee. Whether that barrister was Purves is not known. What is known is that she ended up with O'Loghlen, who had little time to prepare given the minimal fee payable via the court appointment.

In the dock, Heffernan looked barely able to breathe. She clutched the rail, fingers stiff and bloodless, her lips moving without sound. Finlayson would have taken no pleasure in it. But an innocent child had been drowned, and it was his duty to prosecute her fairly, without fear or favour.

Decades ago, Sir Bryan O'Loghlen QC had been a force to be reckoned with. Now, he seemed more suited to a quiet retirement in a leather armchair than to the brutal cut-and-thrust of the Criminal Court.

O'Loghlen's arguments were slow and ponderous. His rhetorical flourishes, once razor-sharp, now had the dull edge of an old butter knife.

When the time came to present Heffernan's insanity defence, O'Loghlen lifted his head from his brief, cleared his throat like an old clergyman before a funeral sermon, and declared that this was one of the saddest cases he had ever seen. Then, with a weak wave of his hand, he gestured at the terrified, trembling girl in the dock. 'Just look at her,' he implored the jury. 'Judge her sanity for yourselves.'

As a defence, it was woeful. Under strict legal requirements, the burden rested on the defence to prove that the accused was of unsound mind at the time of the offence. That meant expert medical evidence, reports, prior diagnoses—something. But O'Loghlen had offered nothing. Worse still, he had invited the jury to assess her condition upon the day of the trial, not on the day she took her baby down to the Yarra.

Finlayson didn't need to object. Justice Hodges did it for him. 'Do not be swayed by how she presents today,' he instructed, voice clipped, tone cool. What mattered, he told the jury, was her mental state on 16 January—the day she had drowned her child.

Almost by accident, the final blow landed.

Justice Hodges, an exacting and practical man, asked Dr Stawell, the medical officer who had conducted the autopsy, whether Heffernan could have recounted her actions in such detail in her police statement if she had been suffering from 'a temporary mania to which women were liable.'

Dr Stawell was unequivocal. 'No. She would not.' In his considered professional opinion, Heffernan was sane.

In summing up, Justice Hodges was firm. Yes, the case was tragic. Yes, Heffernan was young, desperate, and 'hard-pressed.' But none of that changed the legal position. The issue was straightforward: Had she knowingly carried her child to the river and drowned him?

Hodges addressed the jury without sentiment, telling them that Heffernan's own words, her precise, step-by-step description of her actions to the police, showed she knew exactly what she was doing. 'If women were to be excused for murder simply because of distress,' he warned, 'that would be a very frequent excuse indeed.'

Finlayson watched as the jury filed out, their deliberations beginning. He folded his arms, waiting.

He glanced at the clock. They had only been out a short while, and they were already coming back. *Quick juries convict, slow juries acquit.*

Finlayson sat straighter, bracing for the word 'guilty.' But instead, the foreman cleared his throat. 'Your Honour, may we return a verdict of manslaughter?' They were wavering. Looking for a way out.

Hodges didn't hesitate. 'No,' he declared. 'If the accused intentionally drowned her child, the law provides only one verdict: Murder.'

Finlayson must surely have agreed. It was the correct legal view. No emotion, no sentimentality, just the application of the law to the facts.

The jury retired again.

This time, they would return with the right answer.

Finlayson felt no satisfaction as the verdict was read. The jury had done its duty. The law had taken its course.

Maggie Heffernan's body stiffened, her breath coming in shallow gasps as the courtroom closed in around her. The dock rail bit into her palms as her fingers clutched it tighter and tighter.

Justice Hodges reached for the black cap.

The courtroom recoiled in silence. The ritual was stark, absolute.

Maggie's lips parted, but no sound came. Her body jerked, as if trying to wake from a nightmare.

'The sentence of the Court is that you be taken from this place—'

The words faded beneath the roar in her ears.

As Hodges reached the final, awful words … 'and hanged by the neck until you are dead' Maggie's body gave out. She crumpled where she stood, knees buckling, head snapping back as the warders rushed to catch her. She was unconscious before she hit the floor.

CHAPTER 60

On 21 March 1900, Dr Henry O'Hara walked into the meeting of the Victorian Chapter of the British Medical Association like a man approaching his own execution.

The members were gathered to vote on a motion to expel him for his involvement with Silenette Proprietary Limited.

O'Hara had a well-known history of violence. Dubbed by some as *that volatile Irishman*, he had publicly assaulted men who crossed him, more than once, and in broad daylight. The British Medical Association had looked the other way. But when he invented a contraceptive? That was clearly a bridge too far.

Only weeks earlier, O'Hara had walked his eldest daughter down the aisle at St Mary's Church. The bride beamed, the choir sang. And not one of the newspapers reporting on the fashionable society wedding mentioned that both fathers of the happy couple, Dr Henry O'Hara and Mr Andrew Rowan, were now publicly disgraced. O'Hara through Silenette, Rowan through the financial improprieties laid bare in Flanagan's little pamphlet. Another reminder that elite Melbourne still looked after its own.

No attendance record survives from the Chapter meeting that day. But it is likely the chamber was no longer the all-male preserve it had once been.

By 1900, the medical profession in Melbourne was changing. Pioneering women like the Stone sisters were starting to crack the glass ceiling. Dr Constance Stone, having been denied entry to the University of Melbourne's medical school, pursued her studies abroad, earning her MD in 1888.

Her sister Clara then became one of the first women admitted to medical school locally, graduating in 1891. Together they ran a private practice, and were instrumental in founding the Queen Victoria Hospital for Women and Children in 1896.

These formidable women, and others who followed, perhaps stood in that very chamber ready to cast their votes alongside their male colleagues. The irony would not have been lost on them that they still had no right to vote in Parliamentary elections.

The President opened the meeting. The motion to expel Dr O'Hara, he explained, required a seventy-five percent majority of votes to be passed.

One by one, the damning documents were produced. O'Hara's signature on Silenette contracts, his name on patent filings, a statutory declaration identifying him as the inventor. In the company books of Silenette Proprietary Limited, his name appeared in each and every iteration of the Register of Shareholders.

O'Hara gave a mealy-mouthed defence. He claimed that he hadn't read the documents, that someone else had developed the technology, that he hadn't known he was a major shareholder. It was unconvincing to the point of absurdity.

The President rose. 'We will now vote on the motion to expel Dr O'Hara. Those in favour?'

Hands went up.

'Those against?' More than expected. A pause. A count.

'Forty-four in favour. Thirty-four against. The statutory three-quarters majority has not been achieved. The motion fails.'

The President conferred with his fellow Councillors, then rose again, his voice now cold and clipped. 'Ladies and gentlemen, the main object of this Association, as you are aware, is to uphold the honour of the profession. I regret to find that its members do not consider the honour of the profession worth upholding.'

O'Hara barely heard him.

'This Council has done what it considers to be its duty,' the President continued. 'And as the members apparently have no confidence in it, the Councillors now very reluctantly tender their resignations.'

O'Hara watched as they filed out, heads high with wounded dignity. He had survived. But something deeper had shifted.

For those who voted against the motion, the scandal wasn't Silenette. It was the sanctimony.

Doctors, and especially those at the Queen Victoria Hospital, saw firsthand the brutal consequences of unwanted pregnancy. They treated women maimed by back-alley abortions. They consoled mothers terrified of another mouth to feed. Perhaps, too, the news of Maggie Heffernan's death sentence still lingered in their minds.

The vote hadn't failed because the members believed O'Hara's cobbled-together defence.

It failed because the old certainties were no longer certain.

CHAPTER 61

In the quiet of his rooms, Finlayson began the solemn ritual. He fastened the stiff white collar around his neck and adjusted the crisp cotton bands over his freshly pressed shirtfront. His black court coat followed, long, tailored and ornate. Over this, he draped his new silk gown, its folds cascading like ink poured from a jar. Finally, he placed the horsehair wig on his head, its pale curls circling his brow, completing the transformation.

He passed through the Crown Law Offices, the air hushed and reverent with morning purpose. High windows filtered the early light into blades of gold across the stone. He stepped out through the arched portico and turned left onto Lonsdale Street, beginning the short walk toward the entrance to the Supreme Court building. He had prosecuted two capital trials already that year—each solemn, each final—and now, the third: Kathleen Fraser. The most public. The most perilous. The moment he would again face his nemesis, James Liddell Purves QC.

Decades earlier, in the Yarrowee Masonic Lodge, Finlayson had spoken of the law as a reflection of eternal principle, an earthly echo of moral geometry. Justice was not a show, but a system. Not performance, but principle. Not emotion, but exactitude.

As he turned from Lonsdale into William Street, his consecration was complete.

He wasn't dressed—he was armoured. His silk gown billowed like a battle standard. His wig framed his face like a helm. This was no costume. This was calling.

The Temple was not in Jerusalem. It was here in Melbourne, hewn in solid sandstone.

Ahead, the crowd had begun to gather. An assortment of reporters, society ladies and working men. They shifted and murmured with anticipation as he passed.

Non nobis, Domine, non nobis, sed nomini tuo da gloriam.

The old Templar creed was now both prayer and purpose: *Not unto us, O Lord, not unto us, but to Your Name give glory.*

A brother knight in wig and gown, he didn't come to win.

He came to guard the gate.

Supreme Court of Victoria, William Street entrance
– From Victoria State Library collection

CHAPTER 62

Inside the Courtroom, Finlayson greeted Mr Guiness, the Crown Solicitor. He then nodded his respects to Purves and Dethridge, the highest profile and most expensive combination of senior and junior counsel at the Victorian bar. A vaudeville impresario and his fresh-faced understudy, they were rehearsed to perfection and desperate to steal the limelight.

Whilst the Prosecution's case was strong, perhaps the strongest out of the three, Finlayson remained cautious. Compared to the bungling counsel for Foster and Heffernan, Purves and Dethridge were in another league.

The spectators, mostly women, filled every available seat in the gallery, eager to witness the trial that had gripped the colonies.

When Mrs Kathleen Fraser stepped into the courtroom, all eyes in the public gallery followed her, as if drawn by an invisible thread. She moved with a calculated grace, her expression serene as Mr Hale Budd escorted her to the dock. As always, her attire was flawless. *The Geelong Advertiser* noted approvingly that her black dress 'showed off her neat figure' while the *Kalgoorlie Miner*, never one for subtlety, ran with the headline, 'Lovely Woman.'

Today, on the most important stage of her life, she had elevated her costume. Her dark ensemble was punctuated by a flamboyant black feather boa, and, perhaps inspired by King O'Malley, a flowing cape that billowed behind her with each step. If Purves was the theatrical maestro, then Mrs Fraser was now his protégé, playing to the jury with studied elegance.

The sharp rap of the Court Crier's staff broke the stillness, his voice cutting through the murmur of whispered conversations.

'Silence! All stand in court!'

Barristers, solicitors, clerks and spectators rose in unison, the rustle of robes and shuffling of feet filling the air.

The heavy oak doors at the rear of the room creaked open, and the judge entered. His red robes, trimmed with white ermine, flowed behind him as he strode to the bench. He settled into his high-backed chair, his full-bottomed judicial wig lending solemnity to a bearded, intelligent face.

The Court Crier raised his staff again. 'His Honour, Mr Justice A'Beckett, presiding in the Supreme Court of Victoria.'

Justice Thomas A'Beckett sat upon the bench like a regal lion. As was his habit, he rarely met the eyes of the lawyers or the accused. Instead, his piercing gaze settled on an indeterminate point in the far corner of the courtroom, as if occupied by some private intellectual exercise, detached from the noise of mere mortals.

The son of a lawyer and politician, A'Beckett had an elite legal pedigree. Born in England in 1836, he had been called to the bar at Lincoln's Inn, and admitted to practice in Victoria soon after. He accepted a seat on the bench in 1886. But the distinguished judge still wasn't the biggest dog in the A'Beckett pack. His uncle, Sir William A'Beckett, gained legendary status as the first Chief Justice of Victoria when the colony separated from New South Wales in 1851. Another relative, Gilbert A'Beckett, was the famous English barrister and journalist best known as the author of *The Comic History of England* and *The Comic Blackstone*. In the grand A'Beckett lineage, even the learned Justice Thomas was more footnote than headline.

'Be seated,' A'Beckett commanded. The room obeyed as one.

Purves, of course, had history with A'Beckett.

One oft-repeated tale from bar speech nights recounted how, when cross-examined by Purves, a witness had said something offensive to him which was inaudible to A'Beckett. Purves protested to the Judge, looking for him to discipline the man. 'Your Honour, the witness mumbled something to the effect that I was a rude, bullying barrister,' Purves said. A'Beckett asked the witness if that was true. The witness admitted that he had made the comment, adding that it was justified. 'Well,' said A'Beckett with judicial deadpan, 'you mustn't mumble. You really must not mumble.'

The Court Clerk stepped forward, the charged atmosphere giving his words weight. 'The Supreme Court of Victoria is now in session. The case of the Crown versus Mrs Kathleen Fraser.' He paused, glancing toward the dock where Mrs Fraser stood, then turning his attention back to the judge. 'May it please Your Honour, this is a criminal trial on indictment.'

A'Beckett's gaze flickered to the defendant before returning to its usual spot in the back corner of the room. 'Proceed.'

The Clerk then read out Mrs Fraser's charges. The first charge was for wounding with attempt to murder her husband, Dr Paul Wilkes Fraser, an offence punishable by death. The second, less severe charge was for causing serious bodily harm with intent.

When asked how she pleaded to each charge, she didn't hesitate: 'Not guilty.'

Her words hung in the air like a challenge.

The clerk gave a small nod. All eyes turned to the Judge, who leaned forward in his chair.

'Let the trial commence.'

1. Chief Justice's Private Room. 2. Practice Court. 3. County Court. 4. Arcade (upper floor). 5. Angle Vestibule. 6. Barristers' Room. 7. Criminal Court.

Inside the Supreme Court Building

CHAPTER 63

A large pool of potential jurors had been called to Court that morning. Only twelve would ultimately be needed, but because Mrs Fraser was charged with a capital crime, her lawyers had up to twenty peremptory challenges available. This meant they had the right to disqualify up to twenty jurors without having to give a reason.

Finlayson, on the other hand, could only challenge for cause. That meant he needed a valid reason, such as the juror being related to the defendant, having expressed a prejudicial opinion, or holding a personal interest in the outcome.

The jury pool was a sea of middle-aged and elderly men. This was inevitable given the narrow requirements of the *Juries Act* of 1890. To qualify, potential jurors had to be male, at least twenty-one years of age, a natural born or naturalised subject of the Queen, or an alien having been domiciled in Victoria for at least ten years. They also had to fulfil the property qualification, being a *householder* who either owned or rented property with a rateable value of at least twenty pounds. It was an effective way to disenfranchise itinerants, aborigines and the dirt poor.

The Clerk's fingers brushed the edge of a wooden box that had been pre-prepared by the sheriff. The box was filled with little square cards, each one marked with the name, address and occupation of a prospective juror.

'Let us proceed with empanelling the jury,' the Clerk announced, his eyes scanning the bar table. Purves and Finlayson each nodded. The Clerk then drew out the first card and read aloud the name, address and occupation written on it.

An elderly man, dressed in a smart frock coat, made his way to the front of the room and started to stride towards the jury box.

'Challenge,' rang out a voice, loud and clear, but not from the bar table.

It came from the dock. And it had a Devonshire accent.

A low stir moved through the gallery as all eyes turned to Mrs Fraser, standing tall in her black dress, cape and veil. It was she who had issued the command.

The dismissed juror froze, turned and marched from the courtroom. The ladies in the gallery gasped, thrilled by the audacity of it all.

Purves and Dethridge lounged back in their seats. This had been planned all along.

Like the dealer in a high-stakes poker game, the Clerk then continued to flip over cards one by one, each one potentially an Ace or a Joker in disguise.

Kathleen Fraser was now in complete control. She stood up straight and confident, challenging nine jurors after their names were called. In accordance with the rules, she needed to be lightning quick, issuing the challenge in the modicum of time between the juror being called and him taking his seat in the jury box. If the juror sat down before she challenged him, it was too late. There was no *voir dire*, just *voir*. Mrs Fraser had to rely on just their names, occupations, addresses, and her own intuition based on their look and demeanour.

Her lawyers never intervened.

The public gallery watched in awe as this young, attractive woman stood tall in her darkest hour, telling nine men they were unfit to judge her. In a courtroom where women could neither serve as jurors nor practise as lawyers, it was a feminist act, delivered with theatrical precision.

Each of the men challenged by Mrs Fraser had something in common: they were all elderly. A demographic unlikely to indulge a rich young woman's sob story.

By the time the final twelve were sworn in, a cohort of predominantly middle-aged blue-collar workers remained. Their occupations were baker, brickmaker, upholsterer, bootmaker, dairyman, commercial traveller, iron moulder, fruiterer, fellmonger, boilermaker, and two grocers. Most of them hailed from Melbourne's working-class suburbs of Fitzroy, North Melbourne, Prahran, and Richmond.

Mrs Fraser's social inferiors now held her life in their calloused hands.

CHAPTER 64

Finlayson didn't object when Purves asked permission for Mrs Fraser to sit in the dock.

Just like the other times, he smiled and nodded his assent. A lapse in decorum would hand his opponent a gift-wrapped advantage. You could try a lady for attempted murder. You just couldn't expect her to be uncomfortable whilst you did so.

Mrs Fraser removed her cape and feather boa and took her seat, arranging her dress as though she were settling into a parlour chair.

Finlayson rose, straight-backed and deliberate.

He began by laying out the facts—facts that had been repeated in every major newspaper for months.

His words were measured, clinical. There was no need for embellishment; the horror of the act spoke for itself. Turning next to the arguments, he made his strongest point first.

'The defence might say,' Finlayson enunciated crisply, 'that the intent of Mrs Fraser was neither to murder Dr Fraser nor to do him grievous bodily harm. However, gentlemen of the jury, please bear in mind that the only means of understanding the intention of a human being is to consider what the result of a given act would be. When a weapon is presented at anyone's head and fired, and the bullet enters the head, one could hardly conceive that there could be any intent except to murder.'

He scanned the jury. He had their full attention.

'In this case,' he continued, 'you will hear not only the evidence of the act, but also evidence of threats previously made by the accused. It will be shown that the accused had said, "I will either have to do for the doctor myself, or get some person to do it." And on another occasion, "If the doctor was to drop down dead at my feet right now, I would dance on his grave".'

Finlayson didn't raise his voice. He didn't need to. His words came like a knife sliding between ribs. They were precise. Economical. Undeniable.

'It might be said that there was provocation, but no provocation whatsoever would justify a human being in presenting a revolver at another person and firing at his head.'

He made no mention of insanity. It wasn't Finlayson's task to prove that the defendant was sane. The onus of proving insanity rested on the defence, and from what he had seen from the witness list, that was not going to be an easy hill for Purves to climb.

Finlayson called his first witness. Dr Henry O'Hara marched into the courtroom. With the build of a shearer and the bearing of a cavalry officer, his towering presence cast a long shadow over the bar table. A murmur spread through the gallery.

Finlayson knew why the crowd was excited, and it wasn't because of O'Hara's recent humiliation before the British Medical Association. This was a reckoning long in the making.

Finlayson took O'Hara through his examination in chief with brisk efficiency. All he needed from O'Hara was to establish that Mrs Fraser made a clean shot to the temple. A clean shot, by a woman who had often boasted of her prowess with a gun, was evidence of intention to kill. He wrapped up and sat down.

Now it was the defence's turn.

The packed public gallery leaned forward with anticipation.

Not for the dry dissection of medical evidence, nor even in the hope of a new scandalous revelation about Silenette. This was something else entirely.

Every single person in the courtroom knew that Purves and O'Hara were not just barrister and witness. They were sworn enemies.

At last, Purves looked up.

The lion was in the arena.

And the scent of blood was already in the air.

CHAPTER 65

The feud between O'Hara and Purves had been brewing for years.

It all began back in 1891. O'Hara was the attending physician for Mr Henry Snook, a prominent businessman who was suing the Victorian government for injuries suffered in a railway accident. Purves represented the government.

On the first day of the hearing, Purves subjected O'Hara to a gruelling cross-examination.

The next day, it was Snook's turn to take the stand. One of the lingering effects from the accident was that Snook suffered vivid nightmares. He told O'Hara about the one he'd had the night before. In his dream, Purves had appeared to him as the Devil, complete with horns, a body covered in scales, and a forked tail gathered up under his arm.

O'Hara, still smarting from his own ordeal in the witness box, encouraged Snook to share the dream in open court. Which Snook did, to the great amusement of all present.

Then O'Hara returned to the stand, triumphant. He gave his professional opinion—delivered with relish—that the dream of the satanic vision of Purves was a direct result of the accident.

The Court agreed. Snook was awarded £2,000 in compensation.

From that day on, the pair sparred often in Court. Purves was the leading barrister on all the big jury cases, and O'Hara was highly sought after as an expert medical witness.

On another occasion, O'Hara himself was the plaintiff. He was in dispute with a former patient over unpaid medical bills.

The patient's barrister was, of course, Purves, who enjoyed every minute of making his adversary squirm.

'Do you mean to say that you charged this man thirty pounds for taking a small piece out of his tongue?' Purves asked with mock disbelief. 'How much would you have charged *me*?'

O'Hara didn't miss a beat before saying, 'I would take the whole of yours out for nothing, Sir.'

Things came to a head in 1894. Purves was acting for the plaintiff in a personal injury case. O'Hara appeared as the expert witness. Purves asked O'Hara whether a medical fee of five hundred guineas was excessive. O'Hara responded that it was reasonable, considering the case was serious and a staggering forty-five operations had been performed. O'Hara then added, as an aside, that he had once received a fee of one thousand guineas for a single night's work in the operating theatre.

Purves asked no further questions. But when he addressed the jury in closing, he went for the jugular. He told the jury that O'Hara hadn't disclosed whether his enormous fee was for a *legal* operation or for an *illegal* one. He was implying that O'Hara was an abortionist. To be accused of promoting contraception was damaging enough. But to be accused of performing abortions was to be cast into the ninth circle of Hell.

The judge didn't hesitate, berating Purves' remark as unfair and inappropriate. O'Hara had never been asked about the legality of the operation in cross-examination, so Purves had no right to raise it now. He warned Purves not to let his well-known personal animosity toward the doctor cloud his professional judgment.

The former heavyweight boxing champion of Trinity College Dublin wasn't the sort of man to let such indignity pass unpunished.

The anger simmered for days. Then it boiled over.

O'Hara waited for Purves on Collins Street near the Block Arcade. He couldn't have picked a higher profile location. With its ornate mosaic floors, grand domed ceiling, and intricate ironwork, the Block Arcade was the jewel of Melbourne's social and shopping scene.

The arcade was at the heart of what Melburnians called "doing the Block." A fashionable ritual in which society's best and brightest strolled the streets at a leisurely pace, a daily parade of ambition and appearance. It was on the Block, as Fergus Hume put it in *The Mystery of a Hansom Cab*, 'that people show off their new dresses, bow to their friends, cut their enemies, and chatter small talk.'

Purves appeared on schedule, cutting his usual figure in black coat and top hat. O'Hara approached, fists already curled.

'What is this you've been saying about me, you insulting ruffian?' snapped the doctor.

The Block

'Who have you been speaking to?' Purves shot back.

The words had barely left Purves' lips before O'Hara's right fist shot out, striking Purves squarely on the nose. A crowd gathered. They watched as Purves, staggered by the blow, regained his composure and landed a respectable uppercut on O'Hara's chin.

The exchange was brief. Before long, Purves found himself on the receiving end of a flurry of sledgehammer blows from the taller and heavier O'Hara, who sent him tumbling into the gutter.

Bystanders rushed to help the lawyer back to his feet. They took him to the nearby shop of Hicks, Atkinson and Sons, where they brushed down his clothes and cleaned the blood from his face.

Purves walked back to Selborne Chambers to get a new hat, the original having been damaged in the fracas, before returning to the Supreme Court for his next case.

A grinning O'Hara was spirited away by friends who joked about charging Purves another five hundred guineas to fix his injuries.

Though bloodied and humiliated, Purves had been determined to fight again, proclaiming that O'Hara had struck without warning, and that he would meet the doctor man-to-man at any time.

The doctor, meanwhile, kept a trophy.

He'd been wearing brown leather gloves during the attack. One of them split at the fingers when he landed a final left hook to Purves' head. The damaged glove became a treasured family heirloom.

Dr Henry O'Hara holding a pair of leather gloves

Purves rose with deliberate calm. He tilted his head, eyeing O'Hara as a cat might observe a bird with a broken wing.

A hush fell over the court.

Purves cleared his throat.

CHAPTER 66

In the mildest of tones, Purves asked, 'Dr O'Hara, you treated Dr Fraser for several weeks, correct?'

'Yes,' O'Hara confirmed.

'And during that time, did you have the opportunity to observe Dr Fraser's temperament?'

'I did.'

Purves nodded as O'Hara answered. No venom, no biting sarcasm, no attempts to undermine him. It was almost... pleasant.

Purves leaned in, his voice still soft. 'Would you describe him as irritable and fretful during his time under your care?'

'Yes,' the doctor agreed. 'At first he was quite irritable, but afterwards he calmed down.'

'Did you ever hear of him using violent language to the women on the ward?'

'I did not hear it personally, but I was told by the nurses that he used very violent language.'

'In fact, he had to be restrained at times, didn't he? In consequence of trying to strike the nurses?'

'Yes, he was put under restraint on occasion,' O'Hara acknowledged.

'You say there is some paralysis, but the man is progressing and will ultimately recover?'

'I think so.'

Despite his mild approach, Purves had already scored a couple of small wins. He had shown that Dr Fraser had a violent disposition, was rude and irritable, and was likely to make a full recovery.

Fraser's future prognosis had no bearing on his wife's guilt or innocence. But this line of questioning let Purves imply what he couldn't say out loud: that the harm was temporary, and therefore perhaps forgivable.

But why had the hyena of the Melbourne bar turned into a lapdog?

'Now, Dr O'Hara,' Purves continued, 'in the case of a woman of emotional and hysterical temperament, what would be the effect of hearing herself called an opprobrious name and her child called illegitimate?'

The question hung in the air.

Finlayson may have exchanged a small smile with Mr Guiness, the Crown Solicitor. O'Hara was a surgeon, not a psychiatrist. Surely, he wouldn't give evidence about Mrs Fraser's state of mind? She wasn't even his patient.

Finlayson would have expected a woman of Mrs Fraser's means to bring her own evidence of insanity. Purves should be parading a small army of white-coated savants into Court, each ready to declare Mrs Fraser as mad as a hatter. But there had been no notice of any such witnesses, and no expert reports tendered in evidence.

Not only had Purves lost his mojo, he was now making schoolboy errors.

But then, as O'Hara responded, the blood surely drained from Finlayson's cheeks.

'Yes,' said O'Hara without a flicker of hesitation. 'In a woman of such temperament, such an accusation could have a very serious effect.'

Now it was Purves' turn to smile. He pressed on.

'Have you known cases,' Purves asked, 'where women of

emotional and hysterical temperament acted on irresistible impulses?'

'Yes, I have seen such cases.'

Purves pushed further. 'And do you believe that their action at such time is dissociated from their sane judgment?'

O'Hara looked thoughtful. 'Yes, I do.'

'Have you any doubt about it?' This follow up was unnecessary. The question had already been asked and answered. Finlayson could have objected. But perhaps he was still processing what was happening.

'No, I have not.'

Purves was now playing O'Hara like a fiddle. The arrogant physician wouldn't now back away from the opinion he had already handed to his old adversary. Finlayson could only watch as Purves led O'Hara deeper into the quicksand.

'Would you say that the effect of such an accusation—one that calls into question a woman's chastity and the legitimacy of her child—could have the same effect on her mind as, say, a severe physical blow?'

O'Hara didn't hesitate. 'I would say it would cause a greater effect.'

Finlayson may have sighed as he recorded the exchange in the margins of O'Hara's deposition, his pencil capturing each response more precisely than anything tomorrow's papers would print.

Purves then took it up another notch, interrogating the commonly-held medical view that menstruation could derange a woman's mind.

'Are there certain periods in a woman's life in which, whether she be emotional or not, she is less able to keep her feelings under restraint?'

'Yes,' replied the doctor.

'Have you known instances?'

'I have known women to be insane at that period.'

'No more questions, your honour.'

Finlayson rose for re-examination. There was still room to manoeuvre. Purves' theatrics had made a splash, but were in no way fatal. O'Hara had spoken of hysteria in sweeping, general terms. He hadn't once pinned the label directly on Mrs Fraser. Nor had he given any expert opinion on her state of mind that day. O'Hara didn't practise as a psychiatrist. And psychiatry itself was an emerging discipline, riddled with contradiction.

At the end of the day, it had been textbook Purves. All showmanship and little substance. Surely Finlayson could claw back a few points?

He turned to O'Hara and cleared his throat.

'Have you ever seen such a temporary loss of reason, as is suggested by Mr Purves?' he asked, ready if necessary to hammer his own witness as if he had been declared hostile.

O'Hara opened his mouth to respond, but quick as a flash, Purves jumped in first. 'Yes, the doctor has himself temporarily lost his reason on one occasion!'

Laughter broke across the courtroom. They all remembered the brawl at the Block Arcade. O'Hara himself chuckled, and even Justice A'Beckett couldn't supress a grin.

Finlayson knew when to bow out. If he pushed further, he'd likely fan the flames. Better to mop it up later in closing.

He sat down.

CHAPTER 67

Finlayson called his next witness: Dr Paul Wilkes Fraser. Two medical orderlies carried the frail man into the courtroom. His voice trembled as he swore the oath.

As ever, Finlayson handled the evidence-in-chief sparingly. No theatrics, no surprises. Just the facts.

Then came Purves.

Buoyed by his triumph with O'Hara, he wasted no time in making his presence felt. He relished the moment, letting the silence stretch before unleashing his assault on the witness.

At last, the public gallery was treated to the Purves of legend—rude, aggressive, and unrelenting. For two full hours he launched salvo after salvo against Dr Fraser in his trademark bullying, scattergun style.

He landed plenty of hits. But Finlayson, watching from the bar table with a calm detachment, knew none of it mattered. This trial turned on one thing only: the defendant's state of mind. Dr Fraser, the victim, was not the man to speak to that. And doubly so after he had detonated his own credibility with his second Dying Man's Deposition.

Purves hammered him with the well-reported accusations. 'Did you call your wife a whore? Your daughter a bastard?'

Fraser's responses were weak.

'I don't recall ... Not to my knowledge ... I might have.'

At one low moment, Fraser even refused to acknowledge his own clear signature on a letter. 'It might be,' he muttered.

Finlayson stole a glance at the jury. They didn't like Fraser, that much was clear. But that didn't mean they'd excuse his wife for shooting him.

Purves shifted gears, turning to Fraser's surveillance activities at the Federal Coffee Palace. When he grudgingly admitted that he *might* have told the manager his wife was a whore, Purves pounced.

'And yet you wonder why she shot you?'

It was cheap and performative. Finlayson didn't even bother to object.

When Fraser happened to say something that supported the Crown's case, the newspapers seldom mentioned it. But Finlayson's own courtroom shorthand filled in the blanks. The press didn't mention Fraser's remark that his wife was 'a good actress'—words that cast doubt over many of her allegations against him. Nor his claim that she threatened to divorce him more times than she changed her gloves. Nor his chilling allegation that she once told him he had 'five minutes to live.' His flat denial that Grinham was a drunk didn't make the cut. Nor did his insistence that the two did not go out drinking after visiting the Federal Coffee Palace.

Melbourne had long whispered that papers like *The Age* and *The Argus* favoured Purves, because he was their chosen QC for libel defences. Finlayson's notes told the same story.

Purves tried to gain mileage from the scandal of Louie and Dorothy, the mysterious woman and child from London whose letters had made Mrs Fraser suspicious. He produced the letters in evidence, pushing hard to extract a confession. But Dr. Fraser denied everything, and the moment fizzled.

There was one moment of unintended levity. 'Dr Fraser, did you ever strike your wife?' Purves asked.

The witness snapped back, voice ringing clear for the first time. 'Has *she* ever shot *me*?' A wave of laughter rolled across the room.

With a winning smile to the jury, Purves conceded that she had indeed shot him, and moved on.

But now he faced a different adversary: Justice A'Beckett himself.

Every time Purves attempted to dredge up the Frasers' long, miserable marriage, the judge shut him down. 'This is not a divorce case,' A'Beckett snapped. 'Domestic quarrels that occurred three or four years ago cannot be evidence in this case.'

Legally, this had in fact been one of Purves' strongest arguments. But now it was a dead duck. Finlayson hadn't needed to lift a finger. If he had objected, he might have looked defensive. But A'Beckett had done the work for him.

Contrary to A'Beckett's assertions, a long pattern of domestic abuse may well have supported an insanity defence. Henry Maudsley, the respected English psychiatrist, had written that intense suffering in the home could drive women to melancholia or delusional insanity. Even the controversial Sigmund Freud was beginning to draw connections between trauma, repression, and violent emotional outbursts. Freud's *Studies on Hysteria*, published with Breuer in 1895, spoke directly to the kind of internal breakdown Purves was trying to sketch. But he was never allowed to build that case.

Still, Purves wasn't done throwing mud.

In a vulgar move that showed his playbook hadn't changed since the days of his fight with O'Hara outside the Block Arcade, Purves accused Fraser of being an abortionist. The reason? He had once worked with Charles Ledebur, the disreputable husband of abortionist Olga Radalyski from the Boot Box Murder.

Fraser denied it flatly, with more conviction than he had denied anything else during his lengthy cross-examination.

Purves closed with the insinuation that Dr Fraser used to run a questionable massage business. The jury was unmoved.

James Liddell Purves QC had delivered a spectacle worthy of his reputation. He had bullied, insinuated, grandstanded, and entertained.

But from a legal perspective?

He hadn't moved the needle one inch.

CHAPTER 68

Dr Fraser's testimony complete, Finlayson called his remaining witnesses. They included the newly promoted Sergeant Trainor, the clerk from Fishley's jeweller shop, and others who had witnessed the shooting incident. Their evidence was uncontroversial.

Finlayson knew he needed to finish strong. The Prosecution's final witness had to linger in the minds of the jury. This was his last brushstroke—one that would complete the portrait of premeditation.

He rose. 'The Prosecution calls Mr John Grinham.'

Grinham approached the stand with the unhurried confidence of a man who had no time for airs or graces. He was a solid presence—a tradesman, like most of the jury. If his words landed right, they wouldn't just believe him. *They'd identify with him.*

A similar tactic had been used in the trial scene of *The Mystery of a Hansom Cab*, where a working-class witness saved the day by standing firm in the face of Melbourne's privileged elite.

Grinham's testimony was plain but powerful. He told how Mrs Fraser had hurled a chisel at her husband in a fit of rage. How she had muttered threats—said she'd 'do for' the doctor and 'dance on his grave.' How she had coldly declared that another man now shared her bed at the Federal Coffee Palace.

There was no embellishment. No drama. Just a quiet working man stating facts in the same voice he might use to discuss timber and nails.

Now it was Purves' turn.

'Mr Grinham,' Purves began, his voice rich with mockery. 'You present yourself as a carpenter, but that's a lie, isn't it? You're actually a blacksmith.'

Grinham held his ground. 'I work as a carpenter, but I also run a blacksmith business.'

Purves paused. Blinked. Then pivoted.

He pressed Grinham about his motives, suggesting he had only accompanied Dr Fraser to the Federal Coffee Palace because he had been promised free drinks afterwards. When that failed, he turned up the heat further, flat-out accusing Grinham of being a drunk. Grinham denied it, and Purves pushed on undeterred.

'Didn't you tell Mr Gordon you got drunk together?'

Grinham's response was quiet but firm. 'No, I did not.'

Purves persisted. He accused Grinham of being biased, poisoned by Dr Fraser's side of the story.

Again, the answer came steady and flat. 'Dr Fraser never spoke a wrong word about his wife to me.'

But Purves couldn't help himself. His voice rose. His arms flew. He bellowed, jabbed, accused. The longer he raged, the less impact he seemed to make. But still he kept at it, swinging long after it was clear the fight was already lost.

Grinham stood firm, steady as a nailed plank.

Finlayson's pencil danced across the page, capturing every answer in crisp Pitman shorthand. His tidy hieroglyphs, now preserved in the Crown brief, recorded the full exchange.

The newspapers, by contrast, barely took notice. Loyal as ever to Purves, they reduced Grinham's testimony to a few throwaway lines.

Finlayson rose and bowed toward the bench.

'The Prosecution rests, Your Honour.'

CHAPTER 69

When Purves rose to address the jury for his opening speech, he dropped the bulldog persona, flipping into the character of affable jury-pleaser.

'Gentlemen of the jury,' he began, 'you have heard the testimony of Dr Fraser and the witnesses brought forth by the prosecution. What you have not yet fully understood is the life that Mrs Fraser has endured at the hands of her husband. You see before you a woman who suffered not just on that fateful day, but for years, through a marriage filled with cruelty, insult, and violence.'

He turned his gaze to his client, seated in the dock with her head bowed. 'This is not the portrait of a cold-blooded killer, but of a woman pushed to the brink. I will show that her mind was overthrown by the unrelenting brutality of her husband, culminating in a single tragic act over which she had no control.'

It was now time for the defence witnesses. 'Call William Gordon,' Purves announced.

A hush fell. All eyes turned to the back of the courtroom as Gordon, one of the workers from Resarf Terrace, made his way forward.

Gordon's face was pale and his hands trembled as he stepped into the witness box. Like Grinham, he had seen the chisel incident the Thursday before the shooting—but unlike Grinham, he hadn't stepped in.

He mumbled the oath in a voice so faint that A'Beckett had to ask him to repeat it.

As Purves began his questioning, Gordon's voice barely rose

above a whisper. Barristers, solicitors, even the judge leaned forward, straining to hear. Finlayson may have felt the scales tip some more. Defence barristers liked to open their case with a bang, but this was little more than a whimper.

Richard Harris QCs 1879 book *Hints on Advocacy* was the barrister's bible. A well-thumbed copy sat on the shelf of most Chambers in Melbourne. The book urged restraint with nervous witnesses. 'You should deal as gently with a weakness of this kind as you would with a shying horse,' Harris counselled. 'Endeavour to quiet his nerves if you think you can obtain anything serviceable to your case; if not, leave him alone altogether.' Harris then gave a clear warning—nervous witnesses always receive the sympathy of the jury. An advocate who treats them badly risks damaging his own client's case.

But Purves was no horse whisperer—and he had clearly never read *Harris's Hints*.

'Speak up, Sir!' he barked.

Gordon blanched.

Purves turned to the bench. 'Your honour, may I suggest that you imprison this witness for a month? His testimony is tantamount to contempt of Court.'

The room went still.

Gordon began to shake. A'Beckett declined the request.

Purves pushed on, but Gordon had little to offer. He confirmed that he'd seen Dr Fraser grab his wife at Resarf Terrace, but that incident had already been covered in Grinham's evidence for the Crown.

When Finlayson rose for cross-examination, he took the gentler path just as *Harris's Hints* advised. He waited. Let Gordon settle. Kept his voice low. And in doing so, he drew out something more useful: a quiet corroboration that Dr Fraser had not, in fact, rewarded Grinham with free drinks after their visit to the Federal Coffee Palace.

Purves called a few other workers from Resarf Terrace. They testified that Dr Fraser had insulted his wife, but added little over and above what Grinham and Gordon had already said. Finlayson must have wondered why Purves called them at all.

But then, Purves played his trump card.

CHAPTER 70

The courtroom fell silent.

Purves gave the smallest of nods to his client.

She stood.

And with that single, deliberate movement, Kathleen Fraser revealed her choice.

She would speak directly to the jury. Unsworn. Uninterrupted. Mrs Fraser had chosen the dock statement.

It was a calculated risk. And Purves had seen it work before.

Just last year, in the fraud trial of Joseph Flanagan, Purves had used the same tactic to devastating effect. It was the trial that spawned the recent defamation case where Finlayson was dragged into court as a witness. Flanagan, the defendant and Purves' client, had gone on the offensive with a sprawling, detailed dock statement—a blistering attack on his accuser Andrew Rowan, full of financial minutiae, accusations of corruption, and righteous indignation.

The jury had lapped it up.

Parts of Flanagan's dock statement were likely defamatory, but the judge upheld his right to speak, and to speak at length. The only rule, said the judge, was that he must not blaspheme or use offensive words. The usually unflappable Finlayson, forced to sit in silence while the defendant monologued, had shown visible frustration. Flanagan's dock statement had denied him control, denied him the chance to dismantle the defence piece by piece. Finlayson had made strong representations to the judge, but to no avail.

Purves had noted the effect. On the jury. On the judge. And most of all, on Finlayson.

So now, here he was again. Same courtroom. Same opposing counsel. But this time, the voice rising from the dock wouldn't be the monotone drone of a dry old accountant—it would be the trembling aria of a young woman who knew how to play to the gallery.

One of her lawyers approached the dock and handed her a pre-prepared statement. She glanced at it, then waved it away. She would speak for herself. No script. No cue cards.

The next move would be hers alone.

Even in distress, the musicality of her west country burr lent her words a curious softness. Several times she broke into sobs, recounting years of abuse she claimed her husband had inflicted on her.

'I was in a terrible state of health,' she began. 'I hadn't slept for nights. My life has been a misery for nine long years. He has beaten me cruelly, dragged me about by the hair of my head, and he beat our little daughter too. I worked for him day and night, made money for him, and all he ever did was insult me.'

The courtroom was silent, every breath held as she continued.

'I never had a day's pleasure during our married life,' she continued, tears streaming down her face. Her voice broke at all the right moments, cracking with sorrow as she drove home the misery of her marriage.

'But despite everything, I never bore him any malice. Not even on the day of the shooting. I don't bear him any malice now. Night after night, he came home drunk and ill-used me. He left me to shift for myself, went off to England without a word, leaving me to struggle.'

Her voice wavered again as she recalled the events of 23rd September last year.

'When I met him that day in Grey Street, I spoke kindly to him, but he repulsed me cruelly. He hurled vile accusations at me, said he would take my child away from me.' She paused, sobbing, then continued, her words spilling out like blood from a reopened wound.

'We stepped into a doorway together. He threatened me again, said he would take my little girl. The dust was blowing in my face, so I reached into my pocket for my handkerchief. I didn't know the revolver was in there. It got caught in the handkerchief, and I don't remember anything after that. I had no intention of shooting him, none at all. I don't even recall doing it.'

Mrs Fraser's statement had now changed from the one she gave Senior Constable Williams on the day of the shooting. In the original version, her memory had been clear. Her husband had called her a whore, they had traded insults, she put her hand in her pocket, pulled out a revolver which she had carried for years, and shot him through the temple. In the new version, he had threatened to take away her little girl, a statement that was opportune given Pennington's recent callous abduction attempt.

There were then the additional crucial details, omitted on the day in question. She had reached into her pocket *for a handkerchief* due to the dust. *She didn't even know the revolver was there.*

The allegation that her husband had beaten their daughter was also new. Perhaps it was a retaliation to Dr Fraser's earlier evidence that *she* had been the one to strike the child.

That final deviation—*I don't even recall doing it*—was a masterstroke. She had learned from Maggie Heffernan's trial that women who remember everything are found guilty.

What made her dock statement more remarkable was that it went further than even her own defence team had dared.

Her lawyers had crafted a defence based on insanity, but she had gone off script.

The shooting was now an accident.

It was almost too perfect. The trembling voice. The tears at all the right moments. The dramatic rejection of the typed script.

But was it truly spontaneous?

Or all just part of the act?

Perhaps this was the brilliance of it: a performance designed to look unscripted. Perhaps Purves had orchestrated it all, knowing the jury would swallow the claim of an accident only if it came from her own trembling, tear-stained lips.

Or maybe—just maybe—not even Purves saw it coming.

An insanity plea was the safest path. But it carried the prospect of committal to a lunatic asylum. So perhaps, to the surprise of her lawyers, the Lady Speculator chose to roll the dice one more time.

Still struggling against tears, she reached the final words of her plea.

'I would do anything to restore him to health,' she cried. 'I would gladly give my life if it would make him well again. My life has been a misery and a burden, but I don't care what happens to me now. My only thought is for my little girl. She's all I have in the world, and I don't want her to fall into his hands.'

This final selfless appeal was, of course, another major deviation. Back in September, she had begged that her husband would live *for the sake of their child*. But now, her only wish was to protect her from him.

With that, she broke down, her sobs echoing through the courtroom. 'I leave myself in your hands, gentlemen,' she said, her voice barely a whisper. 'Please do what is just and fair by me.' She sank back into her seat, head bowed.

The courtroom was silent. Her words hung heavy in the air like incense, impossible to dispel.

She was no longer the glamorous protégé.

She was the Master Magician.

CHAPTER 71

The echoes of Mrs Fraser's words still lingered as Finlayson rose to address the jury one final time.

He dissected the case with characteristic precision, confirming the strength of the prosecution's evidence and highlighting the holes in the defendant's case, not least the compelling evidence of premeditation.

'Gentlemen,' he concluded, 'you have heard a great deal today, and you have been presented with many arguments from both sides. But the facts remain: Mrs Fraser drew a revolver and shot her husband in the head. The law is clear—no amount of provocation justifies such an act. Whatever may have passed between them, this was an attempt to murder, and Mrs Fraser must be held accountable.'

Then came Purves. As always, his final pitch to the jury was pure theatre.

'I have to talk to you, gentlemen, as men,' he said. 'If you were a jury of women, I would not have to talk at all. If there were any Courts where women were jurors I should practise in those Courts, I tell you.' A faint ripple of laughter emanated from the jury box. Purves' lips curled into a smile.

'Gentlemen,' he said, his voice commanding, 'you have heard from Dr O'Hara that a vile accusation from a husband can have a greater effect on a woman's mind than a severe physical blow. The very idea that her husband would take her child away from her, combined with the cruel and unjust accusations he hurled at her on that day, could push any emotional woman over the edge. Mrs Fraser was not acting with intent to murder or even to wound. This was the desperate act of a woman whose mind had been shattered by years of torment.'

If Mrs Fraser had gone off-script, Purves was adapting with ease as he folded her narrative into his own.

'The evidence has shown that Mrs Fraser, at the time of the shooting, was not in her right mind,' he said smoothly. 'There was no premeditation, no cold intent. She did not even realise what had happened. The revolver, we have heard, was caught up in her handkerchief, and the shot was fired accidentally. She had no recollection of the moment when it happened.'

It was seamless. Too seamless.

Had he followed her lead? Or had he laid the path himself from the outset?

Purves allowed the weight of his words to settle over the jury.

'The prosecution would have you believe that this was a calculated, deliberate act, but I submit to you that it was anything but that. It was a tragic accident, borne of the unimaginable pressure that had been placed upon her by her husband's cruelty.'

In his summing up, Justice A'Beckett made the position clear. The question before the jury was not which spouse had behaved worse. They must put that question out of their minds. 'A good wife,' he observed, 'is not allowed the privilege of shooting a bad husband.'

The jury, he explained, had three options: to find Mrs Fraser guilty of attempted murder; to convict her of the lesser charge of inflicting grievous bodily harm; or to acquit her on the ground of insanity. On the evidence, the learned Judge never countenanced the prospect of a complete, unequivocal acquittal.

The jury filed out.

Now she was at their mercy.

Mrs Fraser sat in the dock, head bowed, motionless.

Finlayson barely had time to stretch his legs before the door opened again. The jury filed back into the courtroom. They had been out for just twenty-five minutes.

Quick juries convict, slow juries acquit.

Twenty-five minutes.

The tension in the room thickened, pressing down on every soul like the weight of the gallows itself.

At the bench, Mr Justice A'Beckett took his seat, his face impassive, waiting. The court clerk rose. 'Members of the jury, have you reached a verdict?'

A grave expression. A clearing of the throat. The entire room held its breath.

'We have, Your Honour.'

'And what is your verdict?'

CHAPTER 72

The jury foreman, James Hooper, stood. His voice was steady, his expression unreadable.

'Not guilty.'

For a moment, time stalled. The air itself seemed to still, the weight of those words pressing down on the room, waiting for someone—anyone—to call them back, to correct the mistake.

Justice A'Beckett blinked. His voice, clipped with disbelief, cut through the stunned silence. 'On the ground of insanity?'

Hooper shook his head. 'No, sir.'

A perplexed look crossed A'Beckett's face. 'On the ground that she did not shoot the man?'

Another shake of the head. 'No, sir.'

'What then?' A'Beckett's voice sharpened, edged with something dangerously close to contempt.

'On the ground that it was an accident.'

The reaction was immediate. Gasps. Then a roar from the gallery, a rising wave of elation crashing over the room. Some stood cheering, as if a great injustice had been put right. Others shed a tear of joy.

Justice A'Beckett's voice sliced through the noise—cutting, sardonic. 'Gentlemen, you have excelled even the hopes of the accused's advocates. I compliment you.'

He turned to Mrs Fraser.

'The prisoner is discharged.'

CHAPTER 73

In the light of the result of the Fraser case, no sane advocate of women's rights will suggest that the interests of the handsome sex are not safe at the hands of a Jury of the plain gender. It is extremely doubtful whether the sympathy which flowed towards Mrs Fraser when she expressed her contrition... and her willingness to make atonement, would not have been counterbalanced by other considerations if she had been up on trial before a Jury of matrons.

— *South Australian Register,* Tuesday 27 March 1900

Following Mrs Fraser's acquittal, the press erupted. Melbourne was as stunned as both Finlayson and A'Beckett.

But Finlayson knew better than to expect legal outcomes to follow strict arithmetic. Juries were never mere bookkeepers of justice, tallying the evidence and returning the only verdict the law allowed. They were something more. Juries were the conscience of the community, and sometimes that conscience had ideas of its own.

The *Melbourne Herald* landed the first scoop: an exclusive interview with the jury foreman, James Hooper. In future decades, the disclosure of confidential jury deliberations would invite charges of contempt of court — but on Saturday 24 March 1900, it was just another newsy day.

Hooper began with self-serving platitudes. The jury had followed the process to the letter, he insisted. They hadn't discussed the case until all the evidence was in, hadn't made up their minds before deliberations began, and certainly hadn't let any sympathy for Mrs Fraser sway them. No, he proclaimed, their verdict was based purely on the facts, and their decision had been unanimous. The revolver had gone off by accident. Nothing more, nothing less. The jury believed Mrs Fraser, and Dr O'Hara's testimony had sealed it.

If *The Herald* challenged any of this, the article didn't show it. No tough questions. No rigour. No scrutiny.

The Barrier Miner ran with the headline 'A Jury and a Pretty Face.' The jury system was a pillar of justice, they acknowledged, but juries weren't infallible. Mrs Fraser, they noted, had every advantage—striking looks, education, and wealth. She was refined, emotional, and high-strung. Her husband? An eccentric, an iconoclast, a cynical fool. Of course they fought.

But why was she acquitted? Simple, said the newspaper. She had used her challenges wisely, clearing out the 'old sober-sides' from the jury—elderly men who might have been less inclined to indulge her. *The Barrier Miner* suggested a reform: not all capital cases should automatically carry the death penalty. A judge should have discretion, weighing intent, circumstances, and mitigation. Without it, juries would keep doing what they had done here, delivering perverse verdicts to avoid a sentence that felt too severe.

The rural press tended to criticise the Fraser judgment more than the city broadsheets. Under the heading 'Melbourne Gossip' the *Narracan Shire Advocate* was savage. The regional fish wrapper took delight in roasting the quality of justice meted out in the big city, commenting that the Judge might as well have said, *Mrs Fraser, if you ever wish to shoot your husband again, do it in Melbourne.*

The Ovens and Murray Advertiser concluded that 'the plea of accident is too transparent for any person of ordinary intelligence to entertain for one moment.' In an impressive display of critical thinking, they stepped through the logical leaps that the jury had to make to justify acquittal. First, they must have believed that during a violent altercation with her husband, Mrs Fraser reached into her bag for a pocket handkerchief. They must then have believed that, by some strange mischance, a loaded revolver was enveloped in that handkerchief. And equally as strange, they must have believed that the weapon went off unexpectedly, the bullet lodging in her husband's head. All from a woman known for boasting about her prowess with firearms.

From Perth, the *Daily News* offered insight from C.A. Smyth QC, a former Crown Prosecutor. In his view, the jury in the Fraser case were honestly entitled to conclude that Mrs Fraser didn't intend to kill her husband, based on the evidence presented to them. He wouldn't have come to that conclusion himself, but he could understand a jury honestly doing so. 'No one who reads the evidence, even though it were published word for word,' he said, 'is in the same position to judge its value as the person who hears it.'

He continued: 'The evidence of a witness may read well, though the jury may be justified in regarding that person as a shuffler and untrustworthy, judging from his demeanour in the box. It is the right of the jury to say of any witness, *we do not believe that person...*even though they might not be able to explain their disbelief.'

Melbourne Punch credited Purves with masterminding the outcome. Noting that he was rumoured to have received a fee of one hundred guineas for the defence, the paper declared that 'he well deserved it.' Mrs Fraser's dock statement, they postulated, had been cleverly arranged and planned from the start. Purves himself never suggested that the shooting was an accident; that point was deliberately left for Mrs Fraser to make. Her statement, they said, was delivered so powerfully that, despite the Judge's summing up, the jury accepted the theory of an accident. This result, they said, demonstrated that Purves had managed her defence with exceptional skill.

Even the supporting cast wasn't spared scrutiny.

John Grinham, the solid witness whose testimony had formed a key plank of the Prosecution's case, was exposed two years later in a country newspaper. The article claimed that four years earlier, while living in a small town in New South Wales, Grinham had earned a reputation for drunkenness, street fighting, and foul language. He had goaded passers-by into brawls, threatening to 'knock them down two at a time.' For this, he had faced criminal charges for public disorder. It was a jarring coda.

Similarly, James Hooper, the jury foreman, wasn't quite the model of upright respectability as his interview with *The Herald* suggested. A baker by trade, later that year he was convicted of selling underweight bread, an offence for which he had prior form. The following year, he was declared bankrupt. He reappeared in the press for a series of questionable financial dealings, including the sale of his bakery to his wife at an undervalue, in what looked suspiciously like an attempt to shield assets from his creditors.

And what of Mrs Fraser?

The erstwhile media darling said nothing to the Press. No triumphant statement. No victory parade.

Perhaps she was feeling the heat of public backlash. Or perhaps she simply no longer needed them.

Purves' leading lady had played the role of a lifetime, and now the curtain had fallen.

CHAPTER 74

On 17 May 1900, *The Tocsin* launched a broadside: a full-page open letter entitled *The Bully of the Bar*, addressed to James Liddell Purves QC.

For years he had dazzled juries, bullied witnesses, and reduced even judges to reluctant spectators. But now, behind the glittering surface, cracks were showing. The anonymous author branded him a blackguard and a coward. 'You are a hired bully,' he declared, 'whose services can be bought by persons of ill-fame.'

Purves made no reply. In court the next day he was his usual self, but in legal circles the letter must have landed like a thunderclap.

The Tocsin had finally said aloud what others had long whispered.

May 17, 1900. THE TOCSIN. 5

THE BULLY OF THE BAR.

AN OPEN LETTER

. . TO . .

JAMES LIDDELL PURVES.

"A sort of vicious, idle, and masterless boys and rogues, commonly called the black-guard, with divers other loose and lewd fellow, do usually haunt and follow the Court."

—OLD PROCLAMATION.

* * *

SIR,—It would be an idle occupation and a waste of words to address you with any delicacy of sentiment or refinement of language. It would be as futile to try and bring down a rhinoceros with swan-shot as to attempt to reach a Purves with a rapier. I shall, therefore, not endeavour in this epistle to conform to the demands of literary purity and good taste, for which my apology is to the public, the blame to you who have cultivated a coarseness of character which compels the services of a vitriolic pen.

* * *

In the profession of law it has become recognised as a legitimate thing that the man who cannot advance by ability may push himself forward by audacity. A Continental education notwithstanding, you never possessed ability, but as a sort of recompense you were inordinately equipped with the blackguard qualities of the blusterer and the bully, all eloquently indexed by your ugly jowl. With these you were soon able to make a mark in Criminal Practice, and quickly establish a reputation as a brute who could make women weep and weak men collapse. But your ruffianly tactics did not end with the baiting of witnesses—they were extended to opposing advocates, while magistrates, and even Supreme Court judges, were not exempt from the insults which, craven as you are, you deemed safe to hurl under cover of the privilege which lawyers enjoy. In most instances you were secure from retort because there were few men who could descend to your depths of depravity, and fewer still who were clever enough to effectively retort upon you and still preserve their self-respect. Still you have half-a-dozen times met more than your match, and then you have presented the most contemptible spectacle of a blundering bully ever exhibited to a contemptuously pitying world. In the courteous John Madden you always had at the bar an opponent whose very *bonhommie*, in contrast with your boorishness, continually reduced you to shame, and you were never known to expose yourself to a rebuke in that quarter. But in David Gaunson you encountered a man with ten times your capacity and a thousand times your courage. His famous but unprintable parody of your middle name drove you to a state of desperation in which you could only find relief in tears. You cried in court like a drivelling, snivelling drunkard, and the world laughed at your wretched humiliation.

* * *

All bullies are cowards, and Justice Hodges caused you once more to exemplify the fact when, after you had passed him up some of your coarse impudence, he sent for the sheriff with the object of committing you for contempt. How abject then did you become, and how grovelling was your apology! You cried and said you were very sorry and would never do it again, and, when you left the court, you got drunk with very vexation. Chief Justice Madden had also occasion to publicly put you down, and again the tears flowed down your cheeks, and evoked the pity even of the criminal in the dock. Another instance in which you received a public castigation recalls the circumstance that whenever other cowards desire revenge for some well-deserved punishment inflicted upon them they employ you for the job. In this you are regarded somewhat in the light of a public flagellator, and the work you are fee'd to perform is just about as dirty as comes within the scope of that functionary's duties. The Broken Hill Proprietary Company made use of you in that capacity on the occasion when Sleath came before them to plead justice on behalf of the miners. Never in history was there a more cowardly and brutal attack made upon a credentialled and honestly intentioned delegate. You were perhaps not primarily to blame, being as you were only the dirty paid instrument of a greasy, greedy crew of chagrined capitalists. But the part you played in that piece of blackguardism will never be forgotten nor forgiven, James Liddell Purves, and, if you have any conceited doubt on the point, just present yourself as a candidate for the Federal Parliament and swallow the result—if you can, without crying or getting drunk.

* * *

O'Halloran, when he proceeded against H. H. Champion for criminal libel in connection with a very shady turf incident, also employed your vile services to vilify Champion in the police court. You did your work so well that any man not so punctilious as your victim would have thrashed you at the first opportunity. Champion's retort was nevertheless crushing, and the public received with approval a stinging and studied piece of invective, which described you as "a hired bully whose services can be bought by persons of ill-fame: a blackguard: a racecourse brawler: a malevolent and foul-mouthed coward: a man whose recent address to the youths entering his own profession was unprintable on the score of its obscenity.

Those tongue-lashings are, however, mild compared with the hidings you have got in the streets, in bars, in billiard-rooms, and on the racecourse. When Dr. O'Hara met you in Collins-street and gave you one-two, you made no attempt at defence, but slunk away to your chambers to hide there like a beaten cur in a corner. When Frank Stephen thrashed you on the Caulfield racecourse, you whimpered and wept whisky-prompted tears, and you once more slunk away into a place of safety. There are plenty of other instances, but this phase of your cowardly nature is already too sickening to dwell upon, and they may be left to be recalled by your own sense of bitter shame. The wonder is that in spite of all these things people are still frightened of you, and even pretend to treat you with respect. In most instances it is fear that compels affection. You are retained as leading counsel for the "Age" and "Argus" and that alone is sufficient to ensure you respectable and even flattering consideration from those quarters; and I know more than one weekly journal that will not admit a paragraph reflecting upon you to appear in their columns, because their proprietors fear that some day they may possibly have you pitted against them in actions for libel. This must be very gratifying to you, and I am sure it redounds immensely to the glory of the independence and freedom of the Mighty Press!

* * *

All that has so far been written is sufficient to show in what esteem you are held by individuals. The general public has also shown its utter abhorrence of your despicable personality. The country would not have you in Parliament: the A.N.A would not have you as its President—a rejection which you made all the more justifiable by getting so beastly drunk that you had to be frog-marched out of the room where the Conference delegates were assembled. Your federal flights seem to indicate that you have the presumption to aspire to represent Victoria in the Federal Parliament. Your enemies will rejoice at your appearance as a candidate being assured at the outset that you will stand only to be once more ignominiously humiliated. Your sort is not wanted in public life. It would not matter so much if your blackguardism were but assumed in court for the purposes of your profession; but it is part and parcel of your character, and has made you not only a disgrace to the Queen's silk, but also a stigma upon good citizenship.

* * *

Seeking in charity for some trait in your character, or some act in your life which may be put to your credit, I find it hard to find one. As a sportsman, a mere pot-shot at little birds, you are said to excel, but the accomplishment is so cruel and so in tone with the worst phases of your personality, that it can hardly be regarded as a redeeming feature. I would almost be inclined to credit you with a dash of genuine patriotism, were it possible to separate the sincerity from the advertising element of your patriotic demonstrations. You once advocated Australian separation from Great Britain, but have since cocktailed on it; and, more recently, when you have posed as an Imperialist, rushing as you did to the defence of a few young jingo larrikins at Bendigo, there was altogether too much of advertisement about the affair to be to your credit. Yet there is perhaps one thing for which you have deserved the thanks of the community. It is generally understood that you have at times been offered and refused a Supreme Court judgeship. I would dub the statement a lie were I not painfully conscious of the possibilities possessed by Victorian politicians for doing stupid and even outrageous things. But I will credit you with the refusal, nay, more, I will credit you with exalted motives for your refusal. Admit I am magnanimous, for how easy would it be to imagine motives that are ignoble! But I *will* be generous, and will make myself believe that you refused the honour because you did not wish to see the dignity and integrity of the Supreme Court degraded; you did not wish to make a stain upon a roll of judges sublime in its tradition of purity and honour; you did not desire to disgrace a position which your best and innermost instincts told you you could not adorn. The self-effacement was noble—it does you credit.

* * *

With this graceful recognition of the noblest thing you have ever done in your life, we may part good friends, although it is only fair to warn you that there are other bricks like this waiting for you should you ever dare again to appear in public and pose as a representative Australian.

Q.

We Women.

[BY RUTH.]

The franchise workers do not intend to allow the excuse of "women not wanting to vote" to stand in their way next time the Bill comes forward. They are hard at work in most suburbs, and every woman who is not already a member of a Progressive League should join at once; and if no league is started in their neighbourhood, should set to work and start one.

* * *

One woman came forward on behalf of her sisters on May Day—Mrs. Beadle, President of the Women's Political and Social Crusade. Next May Day I hope Mrs. Beadle's example will be followed by others.

* * *

The value of spinach as an article of food is placed very high among the list of vegetables. Its nonfermentable properties will enable a person to use it when nearly all vegetables have to be proscribed. Its laxative nature is of special advantage to many people. This latter quality is said to be due to the abundance of mineral salts which it contains, chiefly those of iron and potassium.

* * *

We Women want to see every woman and girl who works, whether it be in house, factory, or shop a member of a union, with an eight hour day and a union rate of wages. The Factories Act can do but little with its inspectors and rules, unless the women will bind together and help themselves. The army of women workers is steadily growing, and there's need of unity. Is there no woman, or women, who will take this work up? I shall be glad to hear news of any movement in this direction, or of unions already formed.

* * *

House work would not be the worry and drudgery most women find it if they would only arrange and work the home for their own comfort and pleasure, instead of for visitors. A great amount of house work is outside show, of no use to anyone, and women make work needlessly in their homes in this way.

* * *

Most mothers will agree that truthfulness is an all-important quality, which must be instilled into their children from earliest childhood. They impress upon children the importance of truth, and encourage them always to speak the truth. But mothers should remember that these lessons are lost upon a child when once it hears her speak an untruth. This, mothers are not half careful enough of; they continually speak and act untruthfully before children, forgetful, or regardless of the little sharp eyes and ears. Children seldom forget, and learn far more by watching you and others than they are given credit for. The conventional lies of every-day life—all women know them, and most women think them of no importance, but the child knows well it is not the truth it hears, and its reasoning will be, "Why can grown up people tell untruths while I am told not to, because it's wrong?" So it is wrong, and the more paltry the lie, the more wrong it is. Mothers cannot be too truthful, if they value truthfulness in their little ones.

* * *

A wholesome winter pudding for childrens' dinner is the following (a recipe of my own):—1 cup of flour, 2 cups of bread crumbs (or sharps), 1 cup (small) of suet, teaspoonful of ground ginger, 1 cup of lemon-peel, half-teaspoonful of carb. of soda, 1 teaspoonful of cream of tartar. Mix well together all dry ingredients; if the bread crumbs are soaked in milk or water, rub them into dry ingredients, then stir in treacle or golden syrup (enough to moisten and make a stiff paste), then add milk enough to make it moist enough to suit, pour into greased basin, cover tight, and boil well for not less than three hours.

HOUSEHOLD MATTERS.

Rats dislike chloride of lime, and will avoid any place where it is exposed.

A bit of zinc placed on the coal of a hot stove will clean the stove-pipe out. The vapour produced carries off the soot like chemical decomposition.

Cayenne pepper blown into the cracks where ants congregate will drive them away.

EDITOR TOCSIN,—Very glad to see that "Ruth" in your last issue makes a valuable suggestion to the girl workers to join unions and show their strength on Eight Hours Day by taking part in the procession. If our well-dressed working girls will act on "Ruth's" advice, the Eight Hours procession in Victoria would without doubt be the grandest human show on God's earth. It is to be hoped our Eight Hours brethren of the Trades Hall will assist in this matter, so that next Eight Hours Day will astonish the workers of the world and humanity. After that, sweaters and blacklegs beware.—Yours, &c.,

B.

ANSWERS TO CORRESPONDENTS.

[All correspondence addressed to "Ruth" will be answered in this column.]

Correspondence is heartily invited.

PROGRESS.—Shall be glad to receive report of Progressive Leagues.

G.G.—Eight hours and minimum is needed for country workers, they need to be brought under the Factories Acts.

MOTHER.—I'm wondering, too, why THE TOCSIN does not take more notice of the rifle club oath. I do not know the exact wording myself.

R.F.—We are sick of hearing of girls "machining all day for 4s. or 5s. a week." Why will they do it? There is no need to if they would only make a stand against it.

CHAPTER 75

Let women be wholly self-governed, not the satellites of men, but complete in themselves.

— Frances Power Cobbe, 1880s

After the trial, Kathleen Fraser didn't stay still for long. She ran a hotel in Melbourne for a while. But for the St. Kilda Sensation, life as a landlady wasn't enough.

On 1 January 1901, Australia itself was reborn. The six colonies federated as a single nation, with Victoria now a State in the Commonwealth of Australia. As the new country began to forge its own identity, Kathleen Fraser also re-invented herself, setting sail for a fresh start in America.

What survives of that American life are her letters. Controlled, formal, yet with a touch of theatre, they show a woman still determined to script the story on her own terms.

800 Bowdie Street, Mitchell, South Dakota,
21st March, 1903.

To Dr P. W. Fraser

Dear Sir, I am writing to inform you that my divorce was granted 16th March, 1903.

Also, I am awarded the right to the custody and control of our daughter, K. P. Fraser, the child of our marriage. This, you will find, will make no difference re the arrangements I have made with your father, Dr J. Fraser, of Wolverhampton.

Also, the child can write you. In the matter of the child, I only wish to do what is just and fair, both to yourself and the child. In my past conduct I have always done the fair and just thing re the child, and in the future I trust to do the same. Wishing you all happiness in your future life, believe me, I will remain always, your well wisher.

KATE FRASER.

It was a cool, practical letter, businesslike even in its mention of divorce and the child left behind.

And then:

To Dr P.W. Fraser,

Dear Sir, I wrote you a letter informing you that I was divorced from you on 15th March, 1903. I also wish to inform you I was married on 1st April, 1903, to Mr Theodore M. F. Budden, an English gentleman.

I wrote your father to this effect, informing him that my marriage would make no difference re my agreement with the child. I have always trusted you just and fair in the past re the child, and I will do so in the future. I am keeping the name of Fraser-Budden because of the child; also I have bought property out here, so am having it put into that name.

My husband, of course, just calls himself Budden, but I am taking the other to simplify matters re my property.

Wishing you all happiness, I remain, KATE BUDDEN.

South Dakota newspaper *The Mitchell Capital* reported news of the wedding, although curiously, the article described Mrs Fraser as a trained nurse.

She also wrote to her daughter, now living in England with her paternal grandfather, as follows:

800 Bowdie Street, Mitchell, South Dakota,
1st April, 1903.

My Darling Baby, I divorced papa, Dr P.W. Fraser, on 16th March, 1903, and I was married yesterday, the 1st April, 1903, at 2 o'clock, to the gentleman whose photo I sent to you in the locket and on the card, sweetheart.

He is an English gentleman, travelling in America for his pleasure. I know that you will like your new papa, dear, and I want my little girlie to write him a nice long letter. He has seen your photo, and told me to tell his little daughter that we are going to try to come to England soon to see his little girlie.

Mamma is very happy. I have someone to look after, and take care of me now.

Please tell grandpa that I am going to write him a letter.

The balance of her letter is unfortunately missing, but what remains says enough.

Even across oceans and under a new name, Kathleen Fraser did what she had always done.

She carved a way forward.

CHAPTER 76

Edwin James Corr sat in his polished mahogany chair, reviewing the freshly typed divorce petition on his desk: *Paul Wilkes Fraser versus Kathleen Fraser*. And below, the name of the co-respondent: *Mr Theodore Budden*.

It had been five years since Dr Paul Fraser first walked through the doors of Corr & Rylah, and much had changed. Corr was now a married man, with a newborn son at home. His practice had grown; his reputation was secure.

The tall windows poured in late-afternoon light. In the corner, the trusty Remington sat quiet. The battle-worn machine had seen countless documents hammered out on deadline, greasing the wheels of commerce in a city back on the rise. But now the new Underwood typewriters were coming. Sleeker, faster, and built for a world that no longer waited.

Fraser sat in the leather chair opposite Corr, his figure framed in the golden haze. He looked leaner now, older. Time had drawn lines on his face, but something else had faded too—the nervous energy, the edge of desperation. In its place, a sense of peace.

Corr picked up the document and placed it before Fraser on the desk. The time had come to end it. The typed grounds were plain: desertion, adultery. The date of desertion was given as 23 September 1899, the day she shot him. The petition referenced their supposed divorce at her instigation in the United States, but noted that no papers had ever been served.

Corr handed Fraser the pen. He signed without pause. The petition came back across the desk, the ink still glistening. They shook hands, exchanged a few quiet words, then Fraser left.

Corr remained seated, his gaze fixed on the wet ink as it bled into the vellum, sealing what could no longer be undone.

Outside, the city thrummed its endless rhythm. Yet within the hush of his office, Corr felt a final stillness descend for the client he had been honoured to serve. Not just as lawyer, but as adviser, confidant, counsellor, and perhaps ultimately, friend.

As the Yarra wound its patient course towards the bay, so too drifted the past, its ripples softening, echoes fading.

And in that quiet dusk, if he listened hard enough, Corr could almost hear the first stirrings of a new century.

CHAPTER 77

Following Mrs Fraser's trial, the tide began to turn.

In 1902, Finlayson finally beat his old rival in court. He prosecuted Dr Acland Oronhyatekha for indecently assaulting Elizabeth James, a typist in the defendant's employ. Purves, true to form, cast the young woman as a brazen seductress who had led on a married man. He shamed her on the stand, addressing her by the nickname that Oronhyatekha had used when making his unwelcome advances.

In closing, Purves reminded the jurymen that we are all human. Gesturing to the pretty young Miss James, he asked who among them, as men, could resist such a temptation? 'And let us not forget,' Purves concluded, 'it is Christmastide, when peace and goodwill is what we wish our fellow man.'

Finlayson, as always, let the facts speak. No flourish, no theatre.

This time, the jury returned a guilty verdict.

The age of courtroom theatrics, for so long dominated by Purves, was nearing its end. The legal profession began imposing new ethical constraints, tempering the advocate's duty to be fearless with a rising obligation to ensure fairness. Judges who had once watched passively began to intervene, curbing cross-examinations that strayed into irrelevance or intimidation.

The 1943 edition of *Harris's Hints* captured the shift:

During the last half century there has been a silent revolution in the methods of advocacy ... In the second half of the nineteenth century rhetoric was still dominant, and where cases were heard by juries, there would be appeals to their prejudices and emotions. Attempts to bully them were by no means unknown, and Judges were not invariably able to control them ... The tone of counsel is [now] conversational and matter of fact ... Counsel will make points earnestly, and, if necessary, with persistence, but he will rarely indulge in rhetoric, and he will normally avoid those tricks and effects with which trials of a century ago abounded.

Dock statements were finally abolished in Victoria in 1994. Long criticised by judges, the practice had come to be seen as incompatible with modern trial standards. Nearly a century after Mrs Fraser's dramatic acquittal, Melbourne courts finally insisted that if a defendant wished to speak, they must do so under oath and subject to the scrutiny of cross-examination.

CHAPTER 78

Charles Braine Finlayson died unexpectedly at his home in Waterloo Street, Camberwell on Friday 10 September 1909. He was seventy-three. A bachelor, he left no children—only the last of his sisters, with whom he lived to the end.

He served as Crown Prosecutor up to the week of his death. 'Of a genial and kindly disposition,' wrote *The Age* in his obituary, 'he was highly esteemed by a wide circle of friends.'

Crown Solicitor Mr Guiness, whom the newspaper confirmed had known Finlayson since 1879, described him as 'A man of retiring disposition and of high and noble character. His work was always up to date, and his loss to the department would be great.'

The Age reported Purves' comment that 'it was always a pleasure to meet the deceased gentleman' and 'during his long experience of him, they never had a bitter or cross word.' Concluding that the position of Crown Prosecutor was a difficult one to fill, Purves commented that the role required, 'a calm, deliberate, unbiased mind, and in these respects Mr Finlayson was pre-eminent.'

Finlayson had once promised to return his badge of office as pure and unsullied as he received it. He kept that promise— quietly, faithfully, and without fanfare.

For Purves, the flow of briefs slowed over the years. The new century demanded a different kind of advocate. One who was less theatrical and more technical. The courtroom showman, once invincible, found himself increasingly out of step with a future he could no longer charm.

Purves made his peace with O'Hara. Some years after the

Fraser trial, the two men crossed paths at a formal gathering. Purves approached and offered his hand, asking, 'Don't you think, O'Hara, that we could bury the hatchet now?' O'Hara hesitated for only a moment before he took his outstretched hand. From that day forward, the two were friends.

James Liddell Purves died at home on Thursday 24 November 1910, aged sixty-six. He left a wife and six adult children. Purves had been ill for some time, yet appeared in court just a week before his death.

In an expansive obituary, *The Argus* praised a man who 'was known from one end of the continent to the other...with... the tenderness and kindness of heart that, in spite of a certain brusqueness and quickness of temper, could never long be kept in the background.'

The paper lauded Purves' mastery before a jury, declaring that 'he possessed such a keen insight into human nature, was such an accurate reader of character, and was so readily able to see the facts of a case from a juryman's point of view.' It praised his talents in cross-examination as 'a skill which has not been surpassed by any member of the Victorian Bar.'

George James Dethridge would go on to enjoy a distinguished career at bar and bench, serving as the inaugural Chief Judge of the Commonwealth Court of Conciliation and Arbitration. Upon his appointment, *The Sun* recalled his early days with Purves, describing him as the youngest junior ever to appear alongside the legendary QC. The paper, with characteristic flourish, likened Dethridge to 'a bright bit of the tail' of the legal comet that was Purves. Dethridge died in 1938, aged seventy-four.

On 6 April 1900, just two months after his humiliation before Justice Hood, Edwin James Corr leveraged his experience in the Lightning Judge's chambers to help a new client. This time, Corr was acting for an accused murderer, another abortion gone wrong. The Judge was minded to refuse bail. Corr repeated Hood's arguments chapter and verse from the Fraser case. Bail was duly granted.

But Corr's true revenge on Justice Hood came over time. Long after the name of Joseph Henry Hood had faded into the footnotes of history, the name of Corr continued to rise. In his later years he worked with his sons under the modest brass shingle of *Corr & Corr*. The firm grew, then grew again, merging, expanding, multiplying. Not in his boldest imaginings could he have foreseen the future that awaited his name. Immortalised now in the pantheon of large Australian law firms, the legacy of that resolute Amalgam endures in *Corrs Chambers Westgarth*. Today, lawyers throughout Australia know that firm simply as *Corrs*.

Following the conclusion of the Fraser case, Dr Thomas Patrick McInerney went on to have a brief political career. He was returned to the Victorian Legislative Assembly in the eighteenth Parliament as the member for the rural seat of Delatite. He later stood as a candidate for Federal Parliament, but was unsuccessful.

In 1925, McInerney's portrait was presented to the University of Melbourne, in tribute and thanks for his work as Warden of the University Senate for thirty-three years. During that time, he never once missed a meeting. He died a bachelor in 1934, aged eighty.

Acting Captain Tim McInerney survived the war and rose

to the rank of Lieutenant Colonel. After the armistice, he helped establish the Pretoria High Court under martial law, serving first as an advocate and later as Chief Magistrate.

Henry Hale Budd died in 1905. A cricket tragic to the end, his final request was honoured: a piece of turf from the East Melbourne Cricket Ground was placed on his grave. Sixteen years later, that cricket ground was demolished to make way for the expansion of Jolimont Railway Yard.

Dr Henry Michael O'Hara remained at the Alfred Hospital, cementing his reputation as one of the finest surgeons in Australia. Outside the operating theatre, he became almost as well known for his musical talents, often performing on the local stage. His most celebrated appearance was at the Melbourne Town Hall where he sang the role of Elijah in Handel's great oratorio, accompanied by the Victorian Orchestra under the famed conductor Julian Hertz.

O'Hara never lost his delight in medical innovation. But that curiosity came at a cost—over and above the reputational price he paid for Silenette.

Fascinated by X-ray technology, O'Hara was one of its earliest Australian adopters. He kept a small phial of radium in his desk drawer, sometimes carrying it in his trouser pocket for days, showing it off to friends as a trophy of progress.

Ionising radiation wouldn't formally be linked to cancer until decades later, by which time it was too late for O'Hara. He died in 1921 at the age of sixty-seven, following a long and painful illness brought on by exposure to the very machines he had championed.

The young doctor William Weston Hearne served with distinction as a military surgeon in South Africa, where he was wounded and taken prisoner. After the war, he returned to the Alfred Hospital, specialising in the new field of anaesthesia. When war broke out again, he was among the first to step forward—one of just six surgeons in Victoria immediately to enlist for service in the Great War.

At Gallipoli, Hearne earned admiration for his courage and composure under fire. He was awarded the Distinguished Service Order for his bravery in collecting and evacuating the wounded under heavy shell, rifle, and machine-gun fire. He was mentioned in despatches five times.

William Weston Hearne was killed in action in 1917.

William Weston Hearne c.1914

Following a public campaign and a huge petition, Maggie Heffernan's death sentence was commuted to four years' hard labour. Two years into her sentence, she became seriously ill at Pentridge Prison and was released early. In 1909, she married a farmer, and together they had two children. She died in February 1966, aged eighty-eight. On the cusp of the Summer of Love, she said farewell to a world where contraception was common, and marriage optional.

There was no public campaign to commute the death sentence for John Foster. Nonetheless, Justice Hodges duly referred his case for review by the Executive Council. In his plea for mercy, Foster wrote a short letter, explaining how he had been under the spell of Amy Alice Peterson, a femme fatale who dominated his every thought and action. Facing the hangman's noose, he reached instinctively for the same story that men had spun down the generations: his downfall lay not through his own actions, but through the corrupting influence of a woman.

Peterson, too, joined the effort to save him. No longer the petrified victim from Howard Street, nor the jeering harridan from the courtroom, she had transformed into another familiar archetype, that of a woman who blames herself for the failings of a man. Pleading for Foster's life, she wrote 'I drove him to do the act which has caused all his sad trouble.'

The Executive Council commuted John Foster's death sentence to ten years imprisonment with hard labour.

David George O'Donnell remained in the Victoria Police and was promoted to Sub-Inspector. He was later heralded as one of the finest detectives in the southern hemisphere. He would go on to take a lead role in the suppression of illegal gambling, in which he was highly effective. Indeed, so much so that an attempt was made on his life. A bomb was thrown into his house in Nicholson Street, Fitzroy and destroyed two or three rooms. No one was hurt.

After a forty-year career, O'Donnell retired to Gisborne in regional Victoria, the place of his birth. There, he wrote his memoir, which was serialised in the *Sunbury News* as the 'Reminiscences of a Victorian Detective.' Mrs Fraser's case featured prominently, under the heading 'A Wife's Dastardly Act.' He died in 1946, aged eighty-six.

Dr Paul Wilkes Fraser remained in Melbourne and never practised medicine again. He re-married and settled in the genteel suburb of Elsternwick. When he died in 1946 at age eighty-three, he left his entire estate to his wife Hilda.

Kathleen Fraser wrote again to her daughter Katie, from Seattle, Washington on 8 June 1903:

My Darling Baby, I received your letter, dear, and I cannot tell you how glad I was to receive it.

Well, sweetheart, you can see by the address that I have taken my old name.

Well, sweetheart, Mr Budden met with a railway accident, and was killed, so I am all alone again. There are a great many accidents out here in railways. Not anything is thought about it.

Well, sweetheart, I am studying singing, under Madame Armantine. She is a splendid teacher. I have a room at the hotel, nicely fitted up with a piano. I was at one of her concerts the other evening.

Why is it you have removed to a new school? Does not auntie treat you well? What kind of a birthday did you have, pet? I wish I had been home. We would have had a good time.

Never mind, sweetheart, I want to get on with my voice, as I have studied so far and earn money with it. Study music, baby! This is what I am anxious for you to know, and then I can teach you the singing. I am studying the Italian method now.

Well, goodbye for now, sweetheart, with all my love, MAMA.

P.S.—I am only three weeks by water journey from Australia. There are a great many Australians here. Cooee. X X XX X X All for baby, my love.

And with that final pirouette, the St. Kilda Sensation took her bow and vanished from history forever.

THEN AND NOW

The George Hotel, Fitzroy Street, St Kilda

Grey Street side of the George Hotel,
showing where the boutiques such as Fishley's Jewellery Shop
were located (now cafes / takeaway shops)

The Federal Coffee Palace, 555 Collins Street,
later known as the Hotel Federal (demolished in 1973)

Crown Law Office, Lonsdale Street

Bourke Street

THE FAREWELL IN BOURKE-STREET.
VICTORIAN CONTINGENT LEADING THE MARCH.

The Block Arcade – Collins Street entrance

Supreme Court Building, Corner Lonsdale and William Streets

Supreme Court building – William Street entrance

ACKNOWLEDGEMENTS

The author gratefully acknowledges the generous contributions of Robert Twigger, Margaret McKay, Julie Postance, Viktoriia Riabova, Tracey Harding, Roy Maloy, AJ Collins, Natasha Argenio, and the author's family – Laurie, Madeleine, Noah and Isaac.

Each, in their own way, offered wisdom, encouragement, expertise or insight without which this book could never have come to life. Their support—whether intellectual, creative, or personal—has been invaluable.

SELECT BIBLIOGRAPHY

All newspaper articles from trove.nla.gov.au or newspapers.com

All original court documents, criminal trial briefs and registers, and wills and probates from Public Record Office Victoria.

A'Beckett, Gilbert Abbott, *The Comic Blackstone* (Bradbury and Evans, 1857)

Annear, Robyn, *Adrift in Melbourne* (Text Publishing, 2021)

Anonymous, *Financial Melbourne – The Story of the Land Boom* (Table Talk, 1892)

Aston, Elaine and Clarke, Ian, *The Dangerous Woman of Mevillean Melodrama* (Cambridge University Press, 1996)

Brown-May, Andrew, *Melbourne Street Life* (Australian Scholarly Publishing, 1998)

Byrne, Paula J, *Criminal Law and Colonial Subject New South Wales 1810-1830* (Cambridge University Press, 1993)

Cannon, Michael, *The Land Boomers* (Melbourne University Press, 1966)

Cooper, John Butler, *The History of St Kilda 1840-1930* (Printers Proprietary Limited, 1931)

Davison, Graeme, *The Rise and Fall of Marvellous Melbourne* (Melbourne University Press, 1978)

Dean, Arthur, *A Multitude of Counsellors, a history of the Bar of Victoria* (F.W. Cheshire, 1968)

Diamond, Shari Seidman and Rose, Mary R, *Real Juries* (Annual Review of Law and Social Science, 2005)

Docker, John, *The Nervous Nineties – Australian Cultural Life in the 1890s* (OUP Australia and New Zealand, 1991)

Easteal, Patricia and others, *How are women who kill portrayed in newspaper media? Connections with social values and the legal system* (Women's Studies International Forum 51 (2015) 31–41)

Erastus-Obilo, Bethel, *A Theory of the Perverse Verdict* (2008)

Erastus-Obilo, Bethel, *The Place of the Explained Verdict in the English Criminal Justice System* (2006)

Forder, John Leonard, *The Story of the Bar of Victoria* (Whitcombe and Tombs, c.1910)

Fox, Richard L and others, *Tabloid Justice: Criminal Justice in an Age of Media Frenzy* (Lynne Rienner, 2007)

Giese, Jill, *The Maddest Place on Earth* (Australian Scholarly – 2018)

Harris, Richard, *Hints on Advocacy* (1881)

Hicks, Neville, *This Sin and Scandal – Australia's Population Debate 1891-1911* (Australian National University Press, 1978)

Hume, Fergus, *The Mystery of a Hansom Cab* (1886)

Ibsen, Henrik, *Hedda Gabler* (1890)

Ibsen, Henrik, *Notes for the Tragedy of Modern Times* (1878)

Jackson, Donald, *The Irish Orphan* (Jackson Barrett Press, 2000)

Lewis, JR, *The Victorian Bar* (Robert Hale – London, 1982)

Lucal, Betsy, *Battered Husbands and Battered Wives: Why One is a Social Problem and the Other is Not* (Paper Presented at Annual Meeting of the Society for the Study of Social Problems 1992)

Mason, Keith, *Lawyers Then and Now* (The Federation Press, 2012)

McBrien, Bruce, *Marvellous Melbourne and Me* (Melbourne Books, 2010)

McKenzie, Carmel, *St Kilda 1841-1900, Movers, Shakers and Money Makers* (Australian Society of Authors, 2023)

McKibbin, Sarah and others, *A Legal History for Australia* (Hart, 2021)

Mitchell, Ann M, *The Hospital South of the Yarra* (Alfred Hospital, 1977)

Murphy, Paul Thomas, *Shooting Victoria* (Bloomsbury, 2012)

O'Donnell, DG, *Reminiscences of a Victorian Detective* (Sunbury News, 1925)

Purves, James Liddell, *A Young Australian's Log* (George Barclay, 1856)

Rimington, Colin, *History of the Criminal Justice System in Victoria* (Hybrid Publishers, 2023)

Rychner, Georgina, *The Pendulum of the Public Mind, insanity and activism in capital trials 1880-1939* (Monash University, 2016)

Rynchner, Georgina, *Murderess or Madwoman? Margaret Heffernan, Infanticide and Insanity in Colonial Victoria* (Lilith: A Feminist History Journal, Number 23, 2017)

Shea, Peter, *M'Naghten Revisited – Back to the Future? (the Mental Illness Defence – a Psychiatric Perspective)* (Current Issues in Criminal Justice Volume 12 Number 3)

Showalter, Elaine, *The Female Malady* (Pantheon, 1985)

Smith, Simon, *Solicitors and the Law Institute in Victoria 1835-2019* (Law Institute of Victoria, 2019)

Stubbs, Julie and Tolmie, Julia, *Feminisms, Self-Defence, and Battered Women: A Response to Hubble's 'Straw Feminist'* (Current Issues in Criminal Justice, 10:1, 73-84, 1998)

Train, Arthur, *The Prisoner at the Bar – Sidelights on the Administration of Criminal Justice* (Charles Scribner's Sons – 1906)

Verma, Poonam, *Defense Of Insanity: A Loophole In Criminal Justice System* (Journal Global Values, Vol. XIII, No. 2, 2022)

Watson, Andrew, *Victorian Jury Court Advocacy and Signs of Fundamental Change* (Journal on European History of Law 7(1), 36-44)

Waugh, John, *First Principles – The Melbourne Law School 1857-2007* (Melbourne University Publishing, 2007)

Weare, Siobhan, *The Mad, the Bad, the Victim: Gendered constructions of women who kill within the criminal justice system* (Open Access laws 2013)

Wilson, Jan, *An Irresistible Impulse of Mind: Crime and the Legal Defense of Moral Insanity in Nineteenth Century Australia* (Australian Journal of Law and Society, 1995)

Woods, GD, *A History of Criminal Law in New South Wales* (The Federation Press, 2002)

Yule, Peter, *Vic Bar, a history of the Victorian bar* (Australian Scholarly, 2021)

ABOUT THE AUTHOR

M. J. Checketts is a former senior partner of a major Australian law firm. Trained in England and based in Melbourne, he specialised in business law and today serves on several professional services boards. His writing blends narrative pace with forensic research and a lawyer's instinct for nuance, capturing the human drama behind each courtroom battle. *The Dangerous Wife* is his first work of narrative non-fiction.

STAY CONNECTED WITH M.J. CHECKETTS

If *The Dangerous Wife* left you breathless, indignant, or hungry for more courtroom drama drawn from real history, M.J. Checketts would love to hear from you.

Email info@mjchecketts.com to:

◆ join the insider list for exclusive updates, early access to new releases, and behind-the-scenes notes from the legal archives;

◆ ask questions about the cases, the research, or how real trials are transformed into page-turning narratives;

◆ invite M.J. Checketts to your book club—in person (where possible) or via a live virtual Q&A—to dissect the evidence, the verdicts, and the moral grey zones that still echo today.

Every message receives a personal reply.

*Real lives. Real cases.
Real history told with the
pulse of a legal thriller.*

www.ingramcontent.com/pod-product-compliance
Lightning Source LLC
Chambersburg PA
CBHW060351080526
44583CB00012B/268